Sixth Named Entity Workshop (NEWS 2016)

Held at ACL 2016

Berlin, Germany
12 August 2016

Editors:

Xiangyu Duan
Rafael E. Banchs
Min Zhang

Haizhou Li
A. Kumara

ISBN: 978-1-5108-2768-4

ACL 2016

**Proceedings of
NEWS 2016
The Sixth Named Entities Workshop**

**Xiangyu Duan, Rafael E. Banchs, Min Zhang, Haizhou Li, A.
Kumara (Editors)**

August 12, 2016
Berlin, Germany

Introduction

The workshop series, Named Entities WorkShop (NEWS), focus on research on all aspects of the Named Entities, such as, identifying and analyzing named entities, mining, translating and transliterating named entities, etc. The first of the NEWS workshops (NEWS 2009) was held as a part of ACL-IJCNLP 2009 conference in Singapore; the second one, NEWS 2010, was held as an ACL 2010 workshop in Uppsala, Sweden; the third one, NEWS 2011, was held as an IJCNLP 2011 workshop in Chiang Mai, Thailand; the fourth one, NEWS 2012, was held as an ACL 2012 workshop in Jeju, Korea; and the fifth one, NEWS 2015, was held as ACL2015 workshop in Bejing, China. The current edition, NEWS 2016, was held as an ACL 2016 workshop in Berlin, Germany.

The purpose of the NEWS workshop series is to bring together researchers across the world interested in identification, analysis, extraction, mining and transformation of named entities in monolingual or multilingual natural language text corpora. The workshop scope includes many interesting specific research areas pertaining to the named entities, such as, orthographic and phonetic characteristics, corpus analysis, unsupervised and supervised named entities extraction in monolingual or multilingual corpus, transliteration modeling, and evaluation methodologies, to name a few. For this year edition, 6 research papers were submitted, each paper was reviewed by at least 2 reviewers from the program committee. The 6 papers were all chosen for publication, covering named entity recognition and machine transliteration, which applied various new trend methods such as deep neural networks and graph-based semi-supervised learning.

Following the tradition of the NEWS workshop series, NEWS 2016 continued the machine transliteration shared task this year as well. The shared task was first introduced in NEWS 2009 and continued in NEWS 2010, NEWS 2011, NEWS 2012, and NEWS 2015. In NEWS 2016, by leveraging on the previous success of NEWS workshop series, we released the hand-crafted parallel named entities corpora to include 14 different language pairs from 12 language families, and made them available as the common dataset for the shared task. In total, 5 international teams participated from around the globe. The approaches ranged from traditional learning methods (such as, Phrasal SMT-based, Conditional Random Fields, etc.) to somewhat new approaches (such as, neural network transduction, integration of transliteration mining, hybrid system combination). A concrete study and targeted process between two languages often generate better performances. A report of the shared task that summarizes all submissions and the original whitepaper are also included in the proceedings, and will be presented in the workshop. The participants in the shared task were asked to submit short system papers (4 content pages each) describing their approaches, and each of such papers was reviewed by at least two members of the program committee to help improve the quality.

We hope that NEWS 2016 would provide an exciting and productive forum for researchers working in this research area, and the NEWS-released data continues to serve as a standard dataset for machine transliteration generation and mining. We wish to thank all the researchers for their research submission and the enthusiastic participation in the transliteration shared tasks. We wish to express our gratitude to CJK Institute, Institute for Infocomm Research, Microsoft Research India, Thailand National Electronics and Computer Technology Centre and The Royal Melbourne Institute of Technology (RMIT)/Sarvnaz Karimi for preparing the data released as a part of the shared tasks. Finally, we thank all the program committee members for reviewing the submissions in spite of the tight schedule.

Workshop Organizers:
Xiangyu Duan, Soochow University, China
Rafael E Banchs, Institute for Infocomm Research, Singapore
Min Zhang, Soochow University, China
Haizhou Li, Institute for Infocomm Research, Singapore
A Kumaran, Microsoft Research, India

August 12, 2016
Berlin, Germany

Organizers:

Xiangyu Duan, Soochow University
Rafael E Banchs, Institute for Infocomm Research, Singapore
Min Zhang, Soochow University, China
Haizhou Li, Institute for Infocomm Research, Singapore
A Kumaran, Microsoft Research, India

Program Committee:

Rafael E. Banchs, Institute for Infocomm Research
Sivaji Bandyopadhyay, Jadavpur University
Marta R. Costa-jussà, Instituto Politécnico Nacional
Xiangyu Duan, Soochow University
Guohong Fu, Heilongjiang University
Sarvnaz Karimi, CSIRO
Mitesh M. Khapra, IBM Research India
Grzegorz Kondrak, University of Alberta
Jong-Hoon Oh, NICT
Richard Sproat, Google
Keh-Yih Su, Institute of Information Science, Academia Sinica
Raghavendra Udupa, Microsoft Research India
Chai Wutiwiwatchai, Intelligent Informatics Research Unit, National Electronics and Computer
Technology Center
Deyi Xiong, Soochow University
Muyun Yang, Harbin Institute of Technology
Min Zhang, Soochow University

Table of Contents

Conference Program

9:00–9:10 **Welcome Message and Workshop Presentation by the organizing team**

9:10–10:30 **Research Papers I**

9:10–9:40 *Leveraging Entity Linking and Related Language Projection to Improve Name Transliteration*
Ying Lin, Xiaoman Pan, Aliya Deri, Heng Ji and Kevin Knight

9:40–10:10 *Multi-source named entity typing for social media*
Reuth Vexler and Einat Minkov

10:10–10:30 *Evaluating and Combining Name Entity Recognition Systems*
Ridong Jiang, Rafael E. Banchs and Haizhou Li

10:30–11:00 **Coffee Break**

11:00–12:30 **Research Papers II**

11:00–11:30 *German NER with a Multilingual Rule Based Information Extraction System: Analysis and Issues*
Anna Druzhkina, Alexey Leontyev and Maria Stepanova

11:30–12:00 *Spanish NER with Word Representations and Conditional Random Fields*
Jenny Linet Copara Zea, Jose Eduardo Ochoa Luna, Camilo Thorne and Goran Glavaš

12:00–12:30 *Constructing a Japanese Basic Named Entity Corpus of Various Genres*
Tomoya Iwakura, Kanako Komiya and Ryuichi Tachibana

12:30–14:30   Lunch Break

14:30–15:30   Keynote Speech

14:30–15:30   *Linguistic Issues in the Machine Transliteration of Chinese, Japanese and Arabic Names*
Jack Halpern

15:30–16:00   Coffee Break

16:00–17:20   Shared Task on Name Entity Transliteration

16:00–16:10   *Whitepaper of NEWS 2016 Shared Task on Machine Transliteration*
Xiangyu Duan, Min Zhang, Haizhou Li, Rafael Banchs and A. Kumaran

16:00–16:10   *Report of NEWS 2016 Machine Transliteration Shared Task*
Xiangyu Duan, Rafael Banchs, Min Zhang, Haizhou Li and A. Kumaran

16:10–16:30   *Applying Neural Networks to English-Chinese Named Entity Transliteration*
Yan Shao and Joakim Nivre

16:30–16:50   *Target-Bidirectional Neural Models for Machine Transliteration*
Andrew Finch, Lemao Liu, Xiaolin Wang and Eiichiro Sumita

16:50–17:10   *Regulating Orthography-Phonology Relationship for English to Thai Transliteration*
Binh Minh Nguyen, Hoang Gia Ngo and Nancy F. Chen

17:10–17:20   *Moses-based official baseline for NEWS 2016*
Marta R. Costa-jussà

17:20–17:30   Closing Remarks

Leveraging Entity Linking and Related Language Projection to Improve Name Transliteration

Ying Lin[1], Xiaoman Pan[1], Aliya Deri[2], Heng Ji[1], Kevin Knight[2]
[1] Computer Science Department, Rensselaer Polytechnic Institute
{liny9,panx2,jih}@rpi.edu
[2] Information Sciences Institute, University of Southern California
{aderi,knight}@isi.edu

Abstract

Traditional name transliteration methods largely ignore source context information and inter-dependency among entities for entity disambiguation. We propose a novel approach to leverage state-of-the-art Entity Linking (EL) techniques to automatically correct name transliteration results, using collective inference from source contexts and additional evidence from knowledge base. Experiments on transliterating names from seven languages to English demonstrate that our approach achieves 2.6% to 15.7% absolute gain over the baseline model, and significantly advances state-of-the-art. When contextual information exists, our approach can achieve further gains (24.2%) by collectively transliterating and disambiguating multiple related entities. We also prove that combining Entity Linking and projecting resources from related languages obtained comparable performance as the method using the same amount of training pairs in the original languages without Entity Linking.[1]

1 Introduction

In Machine Translation and Cross-lingual Information Extraction tasks, an important problem is translating out-of-vocabulary words, mostly names. For some names, we can perform transliteration (Knight and Graehl, 1997; Knight and Graehl, 1998), namely converting them to their approximate phonetic equivalents. Previous methods have generally followed the two-step approach proposed by (Al-Onaizan and Knight, 2002):

Generating transliteration hypotheses based on phoneme, grapheme or correspondence, and validating or re-ranking hypotheses using language modeling (Oh and Isahara, 2007) or Information Extraction from the target language (Ji et al., 2009).

In this paper, we focus on *back*-transliteration from languages lacking in Natural Language Processing (NLP) resources to English for two reasons: (1) In NLP tasks such as name tagging, we can take advantage of rich English resources by transliterating a name to English. Our analysis of 986 transliteration pairs from the Named Entities Workshop 2015 (NEWS2015) [2] Bengali development set shows that 574 English names can be found in the DBpedia [3], while only 47 Bengali names exist in the same knowledge base (KB). (2) *Back*-transliterating names in other languages to English make them understandable by more users since English is widely spoken as a global lingua franca.

In this paper we analyze the following remaining challenges from previous methods:

Challenge 1: Lack of Entity Grounding. Previous methods developed for transliteration benchmark tasks such as Named Entity Workshop (NEWS) Shared Task (Li et al., 2009) usually focus on transliterating independent names without properties (or contextual information). For example, "*Kalashnikov*" and "*Calashnikov*" are both acceptable transliterations for "卡拉什尼科夫" (kǎ lā shí ní kē fū) in terms of pronunciation. If we know that it refers to a rifle series, however, we should transliterate "卡" to "*Ka*" instead of "*Ca*" here. Therefore, we propose to ground the transliteration results to a KB whenever the contexts are available.

---

[1] The transliteration systems are publicly available for research purpose at http://nlp.cs.rpi.edu/transliteration/

[2] http://www.colips.org/workshop/news2015/index.html
[3] http://dbpedia.org/resource/

Proceedings of the Sixth Named Entity Workshop, joint with 54th ACL, pages 1–10,
Berlin, Germany, August 12, 2016. ©2016 Association for Computational Linguistics

Challenge 2: Information-Losing. As pointed out in (Knight and Graehl, 1998), the information-losing problem of transliteration makes it difficult to invert. For example, "*la*" and "*ra*" are two distinct sounds in English, while they usually collapse to "拉" (lā) in Chinese, which lacks the English "*ra*" sound.

To tackle these two challenges, we propose a novel approach that links a given name to a KB in target language, and subsequently exploits the linking results to correct transliteration hypotheses.

Name String	Transliteration 1	Transliteration 2
雷诺	Renault	Reno
léi nuò	*French automobile manufacturer*	*city in Nevada*
奥尼尔	(Eugene) O'Neill	(Shaquille) O'Neal
ào ní ěr	*an American playwright*	*an American retired basketball player*
亚瑟	Arthur	Usher
yà sè	*Arthur Pendragon*	*Usher Raymond IV*

Table 1: Chinese-to-English Transliteration Examples for Ambiguous Entities

Challenge 3: Lack of Context. Without specific context, a name string may refer to different entities and thus should be transliterated to different forms. Table 1 shows some instances which require entity disambiguation before transliteration. Take the name "亚瑟" (yà sè) as an example, it has several possible transliteration hypotheses. If we find "雷基"(*Lackey*) in the same document, we can apply collective inference to link their transliteration candidates to a KB. Since "*James Lackey*" appears in the infobox of "*Usher (Singer)*", we take "*Usher*" and "*Lackey*" as transliterations for "亚瑟" and "雷基" respectively.

Challenge 4: Lack of Training Pairs. Statistical transliteration models usually rely on thousands of name pairs for training. However, it might be costly to collect required training data for low-resource languages. To address this issue, we propose a simple but effective method which transliterates names in a low-resource language using a model trained on one of its similar languages by means of a character mapping table derived from Unicode charts.

2 Approach Overview

Figure 1 illustrates the overall framework of our approach, which consists of four steps as follows.

1. Training. We employ a many-to-many

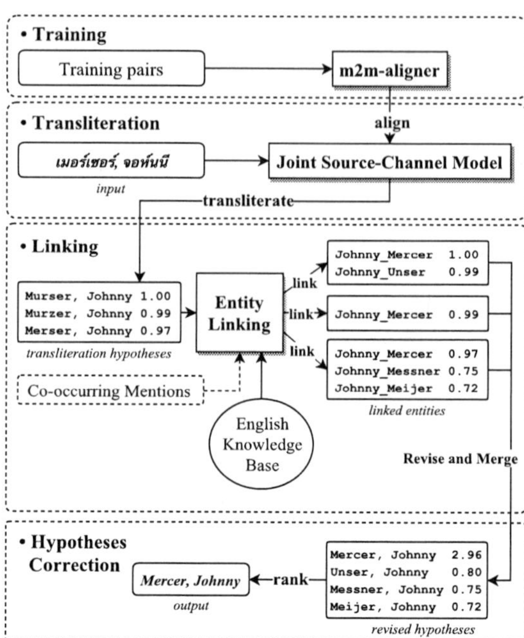

Figure 1: Joint transliteration and linking model framework.

alignment model (m2m-aligner) (Jiampojamarn et al., 2007) to segment and align each transliteration pair in the training data.

2. Transliteration. For each name in the test set, we apply a joint source-channel model (JSCM) (Li et al., 2004) to generate a list of transliteration hypotheses, where the probabilities of n-grams of transliteration unit pairs are estimated from the alignment result.

3. Linking. We link each transliteration hypothesis to an English KB using a language-independent entity linker (Wang et al., 2015). If context exists, we apply collective inference to link multiple related names simultaneously.

4. Hypotheses Correction. Finally, we revise each hypothesis using the surface forms of the linked entities, and merge and rank the revised hypotheses.

The detailed techniques for each step will be presented in the following sections.

3 Transliteration Hypotheses Generation

We use the joint source-channel model (JSCM) proposed in (Li et al., 2004) as our baseline model.

Given a source name α consisting of a characters $\{x_1, x_2, ..., x_a\}$ and its transliteration β consisting of b characters $\{y_1, y_2, ..., y_b\}$, there exists an alignment γ with K transliteration unit pairs

$\langle s, t \rangle_k = \langle x_i x_{i+1}...x_{i+p}, y_j y_{j+1}...y_{j+q} \rangle$, where each s or t corresponds to one or more source or target characters, respectively. The JSCM is an n-gram model defined as

$$
\begin{aligned}
P(S, T) &= P(\langle s, t \rangle_1, \langle s, t \rangle_2, ..., \langle s, t \rangle_K) \\
&= P(\alpha, \beta, \gamma) \\
&= \prod_{k=1}^{K} P(\langle s, t \rangle_k | \langle s, t \rangle_{k-n+1}^{k-1})
\end{aligned}
$$

We can formulate *forward*-transliteration and *back*-transliteration as

$$
\bar{\beta} = \arg\max_{\beta, \gamma} P(\alpha, \beta, \gamma)
$$

$$
\bar{\alpha} = \arg\max_{\alpha, \gamma} P(\alpha, \beta, \gamma)
$$

Table 2 shows that the performance of JSCM on *forward*-transliteration (English to foreign language) is comparable with state-of-the-art (Nicolai et al., 2015; Kunchukuttan and Bhattacharyya, 2015) on the NEWS2015 development sets, thereby showing it is a simple but effective model.

Target	DTL	SEQ	SMT	P	M	T	M+T	JSCM
Hindi	43.5	40.4	36.8	38.8	41.0	37.0	40.5	38.5
Kannada	32.7	35.7	28.1	27.6	32.7	28.9	30.4	26.9
Bengali	37.1	37.8	34.9	35.4	38.2	34.5	36.4	37.1
Tamil	38.5	34.4	29.3	28.6	32.4	31.4	33.4	30.3
Hebrew	61.3	56.6	53.1	54.6	56.4	54.4	54.5	54.9
Thai	36.2	35.8	30.6	-	-	-	-	28.9

Table 2: A comparison of different baseline systems on transliteration accuracy (%). Scores of DTL (DIRECTL+), SEQ (SEQUITUR), and SMT (statistical machine translation) are reported in (Nicolai et al., 2015). Scores of various data representation methods, namely P (character), M (character+boundary marker), T (bigram), and M+T (bigram+boundary marker), are reported in (Kunchukuttan and Bhattacharyya, 2015)

In our experiments, we estimate the conditional probability $P(\langle s, t \rangle_k | \langle s, t \rangle_{k-n+1}^{k-1})$ from the alignment result generated by the many-to-many alignment model (m2m-aligner).

Originally designed for letter-to-phoneme conversion, the m2m-aligner has also been used in previous transliteration-related tasks (Jiampojamarn and Kondrak, 2009; Jiampojamarn et al., 2009; Dou et al., 2009; Cook and Stevenson, 2009; Jiampojamarn et al., 2008). We apply the m2m-alingner to the training data to obtain segmentations and alignments. For languages with a large number of characters, training pairs may not cover all characters. As a fallback option, we extend the m2m-aligner's output with pronunciations or romanizations of characters out of the training data. For example, if the Chinese character 孔 (kǒng) is absent in the training set, we use *kong* as its transliteration.

4 Entity Linking

We apply a state-of-the-art language-independent Entity Linker (Wang et al., 2015) to link each transliteration hypothesis to an English KB (DB-Pedia in our experiment). For each entity name mention m, this entity linker uses the surface form dictionary $\langle f, e_1, e_2, ..., e_k \rangle$, where $e_1, e_2, ..., e_k$ is the set of entities with surface form f in the KB according to their properties (e.g., labels, names, aliases), to locate a list of candidate entities and apply salience ranking by an entropy based approach. After that, it computes similarity scores for each entity mention and candidate entity pair $\langle m, e \rangle$ and re-ranks the candidate entities.

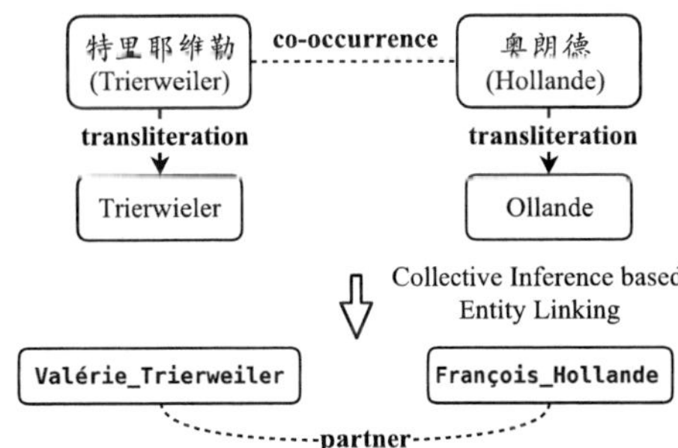

Figure 2: Collective Inference based Entity Linking.

If the context is available, the linker adopts an unsupervised collective inference approach which links multiple entity mentions simultaneously and selects corresponding entity candidates which are most strongly connected in the KB as the final linking results. Figure 2 shows the workflow of Collective Inference based Entity Linking. It first constructs a Mention Context Graph G_m for all entity mentions $M = \{m_1, m_2, ..., m_n\}$ which co-occur within a context window[4] and generates a ranked entity candidate list for each entity mention. KB can be represented as a graph G_k that consists of entities as vertices and weighed relations as edges. Hence, it also constructs a Candidate Graph which

---

[4]In this paper, we heuristically set the context window to be previous and next three entity mentions.

is a set of graphs $G_c^i (i = 1, 2, ..)$. Here, each graph G_c^i represents a set of entity candidate for mentions in M. Finally, it applies a Candidate Graph collective validation approach that computes similarity scores between G_m and G_c^i and selects G_c^i with the highest score as the final linking results.

In our experiment, we first transliterate all mentions with the JSCM. During the entity linking step, transliteration hypotheses of mentions within a context windows are linked simultaneously.

5   Hypothesis Correction

With a linked entity set $\mathcal{E}_i$ for each transliteration hypothesis β_i, we revise β_i using the entity surface form based on following rules: (1) Split a transliteration hypothesis and the surface form of a linked entity into tokens. (2) Compute string similarity between every hypothesis token and entity token. (3) Revise each hypothesis token to the its most similar entity token.

For example, the top-1 transliteration hypothesis of "พอร์เตอร์, แคเทอรีน แอนน์" (Thai, *Poter, Katherine Anne*) is "*Porter, Catherine Ann*", and Katherine_Anne_Porter is one of the linked entities. Katherine, Anne, and Porter are used to revise *Catherine, Ann,* and *Porter*, respectively, regardless of the token order.

We compute the score of the revised hypothesis of transliteration β_i and entity candidate c_j as a product of the transliteration score and the linking score.

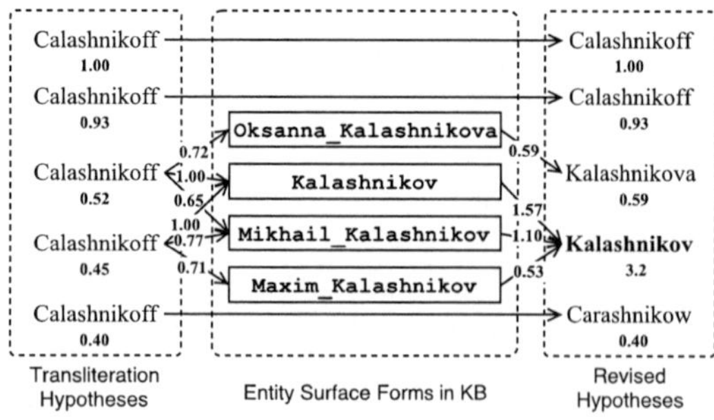

Figure 3: Hypothesis correction.

Figure 3 shows the top-5 transliteration hypotheses of "卡拉什尼科夫" (kǎ lā shí ní kē fū, *Kalashnikov*), surface forms of top-3 linked entities for each linkable hypothesis, and the revised hypotheses. Identical revision results from divergent transliteration hypotheses and entity candidates are considered as the same hypothesis, and their scores are summed. After merging

revised hypotheses, we rank them and select the top-1 as the final transliteration, which in this example is *Kalashnikov* (3.2).

Ambiguous names which refer to more than one entity may be transliterated in different ways. If the context is provided, we can eliminate ambiguity based on collective inference. For example, in the sentence, "在拉斯维加斯及亨德森之后，雷诺是内华达州人口第三多的城市 (Reno is the third most populous city in the state of Nevada after Las Vegas and Henderson)," the transliterations of "雷诺" (léi nuò) include *Reno*, a city in Nevada, *Renault*, a French automobile manufacturer, and *Raynor*, a virtual role in StarCraft. In order to link it to the correct entity, we first independently transliterate all mentions, namely "拉斯维加斯" (*Las Vegas*), "亨德森" (*Henderson*), "雷诺" (*Reno*) and "内华达" (*Nevada*). Then we apply collective entity linking to these mentions. Since *Reno* has explicit and strong relations with *Las Vegas* (another city in Nevada), *Henderson* (another city in Nevada) and *Nevada* (the state of Reno) in the KB, it is ranked higher than other candidates by the linker.

6   Cross-lingual Projection

For low-resource languages, it is not feasible to directly apply this framework because manually collecting transliteration training pairs takes considerable time and effort.

We observed that some related languages share the same or similar character sets, linguistic characteristics and transliteration conventions. For example, a *virama* is employed to suppress the inherent vowel, namely *schwa*, of its preceding consonant in many Indic scripts. In the light of this fact, it is possible to transfer words or transliteration rules across related languages and thereby avoid collecting extra training data for each language. Therefore, we propose a Unicode name-based projection scheme that transfers IL words to their character equivalents in a high-resource related language so that we can apply the transliteration model trained for the high-resource language. This method is very similar to our recent work on building grapheme-to-phoneme models across related scripts (Deri and Knight, 2016).

In Unicode character code charts[5], most vowels, consonants and signs are assigned a name with the following format:

---

[5] http://unicode.org/charts

For example, Bengali independent vowel "অ", dependent vowel sign "ু" and consonant "ক" are named BENGALI LETTER A, BENGALI VOWEL SIGN U and BENGALI LETTER KA, respectively.

Utilizing these Unicode character names as a bridge, our approach consists of the following steps: (1) For a low resource language L, select its related language L' whose transliteration pairs can be extracted from existing resources with minimal effort; (2) Construct a L to L' character mapping table based on Unicode character names; (3) Convert a L name α to α' using its corresponding L' characters in the mapping table; (4) Transliterate α' with the model trained on pairs in L'.

To illustrate this idea, the following example shows how to transliterate Hindi word "अमेरिका" (*America*) using a Bengali-to-English transliteration model.

Hindi	Name	Bengali	Name
अ	a	অ	a
क	ka	ক	ka
म	ma	ম	ma
र	ra	র	ra
ा	aa	া	aa
ि	i	ি	i
	e	ে	e
	virama	্	virama

Table 3: Hindi to Bengali Mapping Table (Part)

First, we derive a mapping table from Unicode charts of Hindi and Bengali scripts as the the Table 3 shows. For example, the Hindi vowel आ (DEVANAGARI LETTER AA) is mapped to its Bengali counterpart ই (BENGALI LETTER AA).

Next, the Hindi word "अमेरिका" is converted to "অমরেকা" character by character following the mapping table. Note that the result is not exactly the same as "আমেরিকা", the actual Bengali word representing "*America*". Finally, "অমরেকা" is transliterated into "*America*" using the Bengali-to-English transliteration model.

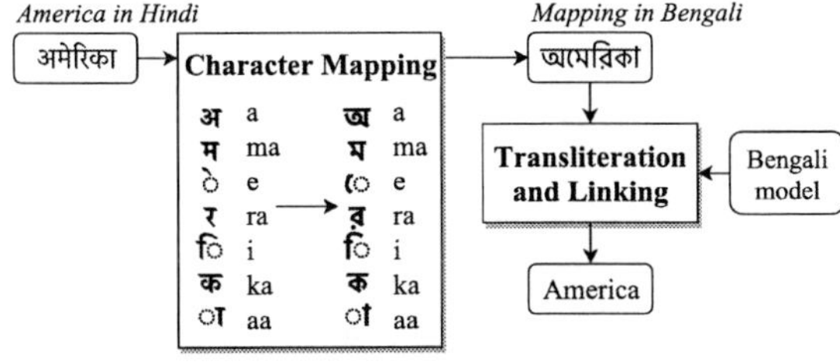

Figure 4: Transliterate Hindi using Bengali model.

7 Experiments

In this section we will present experimental results for context-independent, context-dependent, and cross-lingual projection settings respectively.

7.1 Context-Independent Transliteration

We train transliteration models of six languages with the NEWS2015 data sets and use corresponding *development* sets as our test set since the official test sets are not publicly available. Additionally, because some source names lack matched entities in DBpedia, we also evaluate with subsets containing only linkable names, whose gold transliterations match at least one entity in DBpedia. Table 4 summarizes the data statistics[6,7]. We evaluate the performance based on a strict *accuracy* metric by checking whether our top 1 hypothesis of each name exactly matches the ground-truth transliteration.

Source	Train	Test	Linkable
Hindi	11,946	997	606
Kannada	9,955	1,000	571
Bengali	13,855	986	574
Tamil	9,959	1,000	537
Hebrew	9,501	1,000	924
Thai	25,597	1,994	1,478

Table 4: # of name pairs in NEWS2015 data sets.

Source	Overall			Linkable only	
	JSCM	+EL	+LM	JSCM	+EL
Hindi	40.3	**44.8**	41.2	42.7	54.3
Kannada	29.8	**37.6**	34.2	30.0	41.5
Bengali	49.4	**52.0**	49.5	45.1	54.9
Tamil	20.2	**29.0**	24.6	23.5	41.5
Hebrew	21.5	**37.2**	27.5	21.7	38.0
Thai	29.3	**44.0**	32.8	29.3	44.8

Table 5: *Back*-transliteration accuracy on NEWS2015 development sets (%).

We use JSCM as our baseline model, which has comparable performance with other models used in the NEWS Shared Task. Since we focus on *back*-transliteration from low-resource languages to English in this work, and only Thai has the *back*-transliteration task and data set, we reverse the source and target names of other languages in our experiments. In addition, we train a unigram language model (LM) from Gigaword[8] to revise

[6]MSR India owns the English-Hindi, English-Tamil, English-Kannada, English-Bengali and English-Hebrew task corpora. http://research.microsoft.com/india
[7]NECTEC owns the Thai-English task corpus.
[8]https://catalog.ldc.upenn.edu/LDC2003T05

Source	Name	Top-1 Hypothesis	+EL	Comment
Hindi	गैरी	Garr**i**	Garr**y**	vowel
	वोर्पोमेर्न	Vorpo**m**ern	Vorpo**mm**ern	double consonants
Kannada	ಮಾಂಜ್ರೆಕರ್	Man**z**rekar	Man**j**rekar	consonant
	ಬುಚಾರೆಸ್ಟ್	Bu**tch**arest	Bu**ch**arest	consonant
Bengali	ক্যাম্পারডাউন	Camp**a**rdown	Camp**e**rdown	vowel
	মুসে।লিনি	Mu**s**olini	Mu**ss**olini	double consonants
Tamil	ஜெயதி	Jaya**di**	Jaya**ti**	consonant
	கல்யூக்	Kaly**uk**	Kaly**ug**	consonant
Hebrew	קאלינינגראד	**C**aliningrad	**K**aliningrad	consonant
	שישילוב	Shish**i**lov	Shish**e**lov	vowel
Thai	สกาลาแวก	Scalaw**ague**	Scalaw**ag**	consonant
	เฟอร์ลิงเกตติ	Ferlin**k**eti	Ferlin**gh**etti	consonant

Table 6: Transliteration correction examples.

transliteration hypotheses and compare its performance with the entity linker. Gigaword contains 4.16 billion words, 267 million named entities and 7.4 million unique named entities.

The overall performance is shown in Table 5. We can see that entity linking improves the transliteration accuracy for all languages, especially for the linkable subsets. Previous results on *back*-transliteration are only available for Thai-to-English, and our top-1 accuracy (44.0%) notably advances the previous highest score (39.5%) reported in (Nicolai et al., 2015). Besides, our experiments show that the entity linker outperforms the language model trained on a large corpus.

In Table 6, we list some correction examples for languages we evaluate. Entity Linking has mainly made three types of corrections as follows.

1. Double consonants. Repeated consonant letters in English, such as "*tt*", are usually transliterated into a single character in languages not written in Roman script. Since double consonants are less frequent than single ones, statistical models tend to *back*-transliterate a character into a single corresponding English letter, e.g., "斯"(sī) to "*s*" instead of "*ss*".

2. Consonant. Because some orthographies lack characters to represent all English consonants, different English consonants may correspond to the same character in other languages. For example, "*k*" and "*g*" are usually transliterated into "க" in Tamil.

3. Vowel. The correspondences between English vowel letters and phonemes are complex. A vowel letter may be pronounced in different ways, e.g., the three *a*'s in *banana*, while distinct vowel letters may have the same pronunciation, e.g., the first *e* and second *i* in *ingredient*. Such inconsistency makes *back*-transliteration from shallow orthographies more difficult.

Although entity linking explicitly improves the transliteration quality, we observe that some correct transliteration hypotheses are mistakenly revised due to the lack of context and corresponding entities. For example, "लखपति" is correctly transliterated to *Lakhpati* but subsequently revised to *Lakhpat* because *Lakhpati* is absent in the KB.

7.2 Context-Dependent Transliteration

In order to evaluate context-dependent transliteration, we train a Chinese-to-English transliteration model on 44, 146 name pairs (Ji et al., 2009), and use the Chinese-to-English Entity Discovery and Linking data set in NIST TAC-KBP2015 evaluation (Ji et al., 2015) since the NEWS2015 Chinese data set only contains transliteration pairs without any contextual information. This data set contains 160 documents and 11, 066 Chinese mentions, including 1, 239 person names (469 unique ones). Each name has a ground-truth transliteration derived from English KB title.

JSCM	Non-Collective	Collective
32.9	56.4	57.1

Table 7: Impact of collective inference on transliteration (%).

Table 7 presents the results for person names. We can see that by exploiting the contextual information, collective inference provides more accurate entity linking and hence further enhances transliteration.

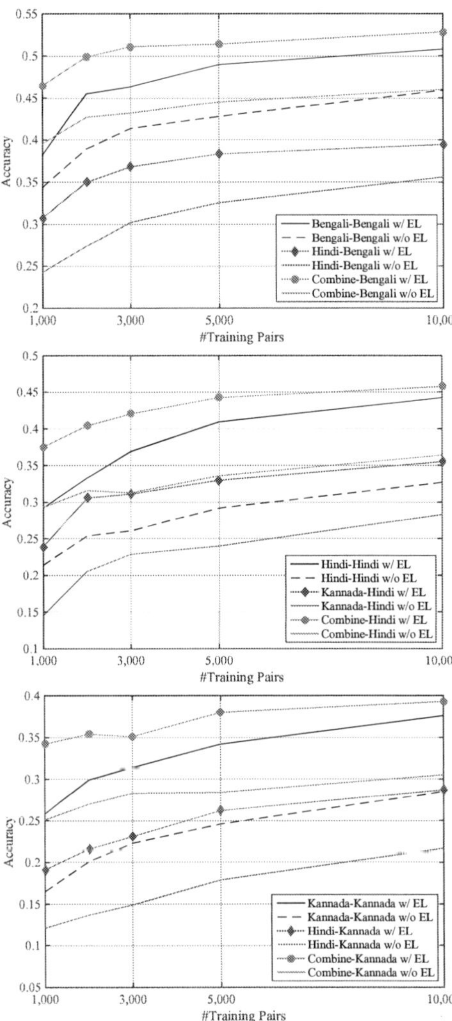

Figure 5: Transliteration accuracy score with different sizes of training pairs. The first language of each pair is the language that the model is trained on, and the second one is the test language.

7.3 Cross-lingual Projection

In projection experiments, we train transliteration models on the NEWS2015 data sets described in Section 7.1, and evaluate each with other languages using the projection approach proposed in Section 6. Among the six languages, our results show that the Hindi model is the best for transliterating Bengali and Kannada names, while the Kannada model is the best for transliterating Hindi names. Learning curves of these three pairs depicted in Figure 5 show that it is feasible to transliterate names using a model trained on a related language without extra data. For example, a train-

ing set of $10,000$ Hindi-English pairs achieves the same performance as $4,000$ Kannada-English pairs on transliterating Kannada names.

Nevertheless, we still observe a performance gap between training from the related language and the source language itself. This indicates that after applying our character mapping-based method, dissimilarities may still exist between the representations of the same name from two related languages. For example, because "भ" is the most similar Hindi character for Bengali character "ভ", we mapped "ভ" to "भ". However, apart from their common transliteration "*bh*", "ভ" can also be transliterated to "*v*", such as "ভেঙ্কটেশ" (*Venkatesh*), thereby leading to some incorrect transliterations, e.g., "अभनिभास" (*Abhinbhaas*) to "*Abhinvass*". Another example is that the combination of "ॉ" and "क" is usually transliterated to "*ock*" in the Bengali training set, whereas its Hindi equivalent "েক" is usually transliterated to "*och*" or "*ok*", and therefore "लॉकेट"(*locket*) is incorrectly transliterated to "*loket*". In addition, representations referring to the same entity may have divergent origins in different languages (e.g., "*German*" has variants including "*Germanisch*", "*Deutsch*", "*Alemannisch*", "*niemy*" and "*Sachsen*").

However, we see that such performance gap can be narrowed or filled by entity linking. In Figure 5, *Kannada-Hindi w/EL* and *Hindi-Kannada w/EL* even outperform *Hindi-Hindi w/o EL* and *Kannada-Kannada w/o EL*, respectively.

We also train combination models using different sizes of pairs of a source language and $10,000$ pairs of its related language. Such a combination dramatically improves the performance, which means that by borrowing pairs from a related language, we can develop a high-performance model with only a small amount of transliteration pairs of the source language.

We also find that it is difficult to construct mapping tables for Thai and Hebrew since they share few similar character names with Hindi, Kannada, Bengali, and Tamil. Additionally, despite of the fact that Kannada and Tamil lie on the same language family branch, they have evolved independently for centuries and have different representations of sounds, which to some extent explains why the projection between them is not as effective. For example, in Kannnda script, there are different letters for ka (ಕ) and ga (ಗ), whereas Tamil only uses one letter க (ka).

7.4 Remaining Challenges

Regardless of our improvement and promising results, the overall strict accuracy name transliteration is still quite low. We categorize the remaining challenges as follows.

- **Name Segmentation**. Some additional splitting or merging operations are needed for some names. For example, "अग्नपुराण" in Hindi should be transliterated into two tokens "*Agni Purana*".

- **Source Language Specific Features**. For example, "*-istan*" is a common country suffix in Turkish and Persian, and thus it can be ignored during transliteration (e.g., when transliterating "*Gürcistan*" in Turkish to English, we can focus on transliterating "*Gürc*" to "*Georgia*").

- **Entity Profile**. Name transliteration might follow specific conventions based on the entity's origin, gender, title and characteristic. For example, "*Monroe*" is transliterated to "门罗" (mén luó) in "*James Monroe*", the fifth President of the United States, while "梦露" (mèng lù) in "*Marilyn Monroe*", a famous American actress, where "门", "罗", "梦" and "露" refer to "*door*", "*net*", "*dream*" and "*dew*", respectively. For celebrities with corresponding entities in the KB, the collective inference method we employ can resolve the ambiguity and hence generate correct transliterations, while it does not work for out-of-KB ones. In order to transliterate such out-of-KB names, some of their properties, such as gender, need to be inferred from the text.

8 Related Work

In terms of transliteration unit, existing machine transliteration models can be classified into three categories, phoneme-based (Knight and Graehl, 1997; Lee and Choi, 1998; Wan and Verspoor, 1998; Jung et al., 2000; Meng et al., 2001; Oh and Choi, 2002; Virga and Khudanpur, 2003; Gao et al., 2005), grapheme-based (Li et al., 2004; Zhang et al., 2004; Ekbal et al., 2006; Ganesh et al., 2008; Das et al., 2009; Chinnakotla et al., 2010; Finch and Sumita, 2010), and hybrid (Al-Onaizan and Knight, 2002; Bilac and Tanaka, 2004; Oh and Choi, 2005; Oh et al., 2006; Kim et al., 1999).

Since names are inherently associated with entities, it is natural to leverage entity linking to improve name transliteration. To the best of our knowledge, this is the first study using entity linking results to revise transliteration hypotheses. We also take the specific context of a name into consideration to improve the quality of entity linking and reduce ambiguity.

Additionally, to tackle the data sparsity challenge in low-resource languages, we propose a simple but effective cross-lingual projection approach to take advantage of resources in related languages. Similar cross-lingual projection methods based on data/annotation transfer have also been exploited for other Natural Language Processing tasks, including relation extraction, data annotation, entity recognition, and grapheme-to-phoneme models (Xia and Lewis, 2007; Padó and Lapata, 2009; Kim et al., 2010; Faruqui and Kumar, 2015; Deri and Knight, 2016).

9 Conclusions and Future Work

For many names we need to know the real-world entities they refer to before generating their correct transliterations. In this paper we developed a novel context-aware name transliteration approach by leveraging Entity Linking and related language projection. Experiments have demonstrated that our approach can significantly enhance the transliteration performance. In the future we will explore more knowledge from the KB such as types and properties of entities to improve disambiguation and transliteration. We will also aim to incorporate morphology analysis, acquire and incorporate language-specific and culture-specific characteristics to address the remaining challenges.

Acknowledgment

The work was supported by the U.S. DARPA LORELEI Program No. HR0011-15-C-0115 and ARL/ARO MURI W911NF-10-1-0533. The views and conclusions contained in this document are those of the authors and should not be interpreted as representing the official policies, either expressed or implied, of the U.S. Government. The U.S. Government is authorized to reproduce and distribute reprints for Government purposes notwithstanding any copyright notation here on.

References

Yaser Al-Onaizan and Kevin Knight. 2002. Translating named entities using monolingual and bilingual resources. In *ACL2002*.

Slaven Bilac and Hozumi Tanaka. 2004. A hybrid back-transliteration system for Japanese. In *COLING2004*.

Manoj K Chinnakotla, Om P Damani, and Avijit Satoskar. 2010. Transliteration for resource-scarce languages. *ACM Transactions on Asian Language Information Processing*.

Paul Cook and Suzanne Stevenson. 2009. An unsupervised model for text message normalization. In *ACL2009*.

Amitava Das, Asif Ekbal, Tapabrata Mandal, and Sivaji Bandyopadhyay. 2009. English to Hindi machine transliteration system at NEWS 2009. In *ACL2009*.

Aliya Deri and Kevin Knight. 2016. Grapheme-to-phoneme models for (almost) any language. In *ACL2016*.

Qing Dou, Shane Bergsma, Sittichai Jiampojamarn, and Grzegorz Kondrak. 2009. A ranking approach to stress prediction for letter-to-phoneme conversion. In *ACL2009*.

Asif Ekbal, Sudip Kumar Naskar, and Sivaji Bandyopadhyay. 2006. A modified joint source-channel model for transliteration. In *ACL2006*.

Manaal Faruqui and Shankar Kumar. 2015. Multilingual open relation extraction using cross-lingual projection. *NAACL2015*.

Andrew M Finch and Eiichiro Sumita. 2010. A Bayesian model of bilingual segmentation for transliteration. In *IWSLT2010*.

Surya Ganesh, Sree Harsha, Prasad Pingali, and Vasudeva Verma. 2008. Statistical transliteration for cross language information retrieval using HMM alignment model and CRF. In *IJCNLP2008*.

Wei Gao, Kam-Fai Wong, and Wai Lam. 2005. Phoneme-based transliteration of foreign names for OOV problem. In *IJCNLP2005*.

Heng Ji, Ralph Grishman, Dayne Freitag, Matthias Blume, John Wang, Shahram Khadivi, Richard Zens, and Hermann Ney. 2009. Name extraction and translation for distillation. *Handbook of Natural Language Processing and Machine Translation: DARPA Global Autonomous Language Exploitation*.

Heng Ji, Joel Nothman, Ben Hachey, and Radu Florian. 2015. Overview of TAC-KBP2015 tri-lingual entity discovery and linking. In *TAC2015*.

Sittichai Jiampojamarn and Grzegorz Kondrak. 2009. Online discriminative training for grapheme-to-phoneme conversion. In *ISCA2009*.

Sittichai Jiampojamarn, Grzegorz Kondrak, and Tarek Sherif. 2007. Applying many-to-many alignments and hidden Markov models to letter-to-phoneme conversion. In *NAACL2007*.

Sittichai Jiampojamarn, Colin Cherry, and Grzegorz Kondrak. 2008. Joint processing and discriminative training for letter-to-phoneme conversion. In *ACL2008*.

Sittichai Jiampojamarn, Aditya Bhargava, Qing Dou, Kenneth Dwyer, and Grzegorz Kondrak. 2009. DirecTL: a language-independent approach to transliteration. In *ACL2009*.

Sung Young Jung, SungLim Hong, and Eunok Paek. 2000. An English to Korean transliteration model of extended Markov window. In *ACL2000*.

Jung-Jae Kim, Jae-Sung Lee, and Key-Sun Choi. 1999. Pronunciation unit based automatic English-Korean transliteration model using neural network. In *Proceedings of Korea Cognitive Science Association*.

Seokhwan Kim, Minwoo Jeong, Jonghoon Lee, and Gary Geunbae Lee. 2010. A cross-lingual annotation projection approach for relation detection. In *COLING2010*.

Kevin Knight and Jonathan Graehl. 1997. Machine transliteration. In *EACL1997*.

Kevin Knight and Jonathan Graehl. 1998. Machine transliteration. *Computational Linguistics*.

Anoop Kunchukuttan and Pushpak Bhattacharyya. 2015. Data representation methods and use of mined corpora for Indian language transliteration. In *ACL2015*.

Jae-Sung Lee and Key-Sun Choi. 1998. English to Korean statistical transliteration for information retrieval.

Haizhou Li, Min Zhang, and Jian Su. 2004. A joint source-channel model for machine transliteration. In *ACL2004*.

Haizhou Li, A Kumaran, Vladimir Pervouchine, and Min Zhang. 2009. Report of NEWS 2009 machine transliteration shared task. In *ACL2009*.

Helen M Meng, Wai-Kit Lo, Berlin Chen, and Karen Tang. 2001. Generating phonetic cognates to handle named entities in English-Chinese cross-language spoken document retrieval. In *ASRU2001*.

Garrett Nicolai, Bradley Hauer, Mohammad Salameh, Adam St Arnaud, Ying Xu, Lei Yao, and Grzegorz Kondrak. 2015. Multiple system combination for transliteration. In *ACL2015*.

Jong-Hoon Oh and Key-Sun Choi. 2002. An English-Korean transliteration model using pronunciation and contextual rules. In *COLING2002*.

Jong-Hoon Oh and Key-Sun Choi. 2005. An ensemble of grapheme and phoneme for machine transliteration. In *IJCNLP2005*.

Jong-Hoon Oh and Hitoshi Isahara. 2007. Machine transliteration using multiple transliteration engines and hypothesis re-ranking. *MT Summit*.

Jong-Hoon Oh, Key-Sun Choi, and Hitoshi Isahara. 2006. A machine transliteration model based on correspondence between graphemes and phonemes. *ACM Transactions on Asian Language Information Processing*.

Sebastian Padó and Mirella Lapata. 2009. Cross-lingual annotation projection for semantic roles. *JAIR*.

Paola Virga and Sanjeev Khudanpur. 2003. Transliteration of proper names in cross-lingual information retrieval. In *ACL2003*.

Stephen Wan and Cornelia Maria Verspoor. 1998. Automatic English-Chinese name transliteration for development of multilingual resources. In *COLING1998*.

Han Wang, Jin Guang Zheng, Xiaogang Ma, Peter Fox, and Heng Ji. 2015. Language and domain independent entity linking with quantified collective validation. In *EMNLP2015*.

Fei Xia and William D Lewis. 2007. Multilingual structural projection across interlinear text. In *NAACL2007*.

Min Zhang, Haizhou Li, and Jian Su. 2004. Direct orthographical mapping for machine transliteration. In *COLING2004*.

Multi-source named entity typing for social media

Reuth Vexler
Information Systems Dep.
University of Haifa
Haifa, Israel, 31905
reuthvex@gmail.com

Einat Minkov
Information Systems Dep.
University of Haifa
Haifa, Israel, 31905
einatm@is.haifa.ac.il

Abstract

Typed lexicons that encode knowledge about the semantic types of an entity name, e.g., that 'Paris' denotes a *geolocation*, *product*, or *person*, have proven useful for many text processing tasks. While lexicons may be derived from large-scale knowledge bases (KBs), KBs are inherently imperfect, in particular they lack coverage with respect to long tail entity names. We infer the types of a given entity name using multi-source learning, considering information obtained by alignment to the Freebase knowledge base, Web-scale distributional patterns, and global semi-structured contexts retrieved by means of Web search. Evaluation in the challenging domain of social media shows that multi-source learning improves performance compared with rule-based KB lookups, boosting typing results for some semantic categories.

1 Introduction

Typed lexicons associate lexical entity names with a set of semantic types, e.g., the name 'Paris' may be mapped into the semantic categories of *geolocation*, *product*, or *person*. Such world knowledge has proven valuable for various text processing tasks, including the classification of search queries (Pasca, 2004), question answering (Bordes et al., 2014; Yao and Durme, 2014), named entity recognition (Ling and Weld, 2012; Yamada et al., 2015), entity linking (Fang and Chang, 2014; Hoffart et al., 2014), and relation extraction (Ling and Weld, 2012; Chang et al., 2014).

Over the last years, large scale knowledge bases (KBs) have become available, like Freebase (Bollacker et al., 2008), DBPedia (Auer et al., 2007) and YAGO (Suchanek et al., 2007), which organize entities and their lexical aliases into semantic categories (or, *types*). KBs are inherently incomplete however in their coverage of world knowledge (West et al., 2014). This is partly because updates to the database with emerging entities and facts exhibit some delay (Wang et al., 2012; Hoffart et al., 2014). In addition, the 'long tail' of unpopular, local or domain-specific concepts is under-represented in general knowledge bases (Lin et al., 2012; Ling and Weld, 2012).

In this work, we seek to associate semantic types of interest with a given entity name. We refer to this problem as *named entity typing*. Our main focus is on names mentioned on social media. In this domain, local contextual information is often very limited, so that background world knowledge is especially useful for semantic processing purposes. For example, the commercial system described by Gattani *et al.* (2013) performs named entity recognition in tweets by matching the tweet text against known entity names in a reference knowledge base (KB). But, emerging and long tail entity names, which are frequently mentioned on social media, e.g., the names of local businesses, as well as informal names, abbreviations, and acronyms, are often missing from KBs (Ritter et al., 2011).

Previously, researchers have proposed to infer the semantic types of entity names based on local distributional evidence harvested from Web documents (Lin et al., 2012; Yaghoobzadeh and Schütze, 2015), however such distributional evidence is sparse and costly to obtain for long tail names. We claim that in order to infer the semantic types of infrequent entity names, it is neces-

Proceedings of the Sixth Named Entity Workshop, joint with 54th ACL, pages 11–20,
Berlin, Germany, August 12, 2016. ©2016 Association for Computational Linguistics

sary to model global, semi-structured, contextual evidence of the respective name mentions. Specifically, we consider in this work paragraph-level contexts, Webpage titles and URLs, obtained by means of Web search. As suggested by Rüd *et al.* (2011), Web search has several advantages as a source of background knowledge in cross-domain settings. We believe this work to be the first to examine Web search as an information source for the task of entity name typing, and the first to evaluate this task in the social media domain.

We apply a discriminative learning framework using an ensemble of information sources, naming this approach as Multi-Source Named Entity Typing (MS-NET). Relevant evidence about a given entity name is extracted from the various sources and represented as features in a joint feature space. Specifically, we model as features in this work related Freebase category tags, distributional information in the form of ReVerb lexico-syntactic patterns (Fader et al., 2011), and semi-structured Web search results.

In our experiments, we consider a set of nine target semantic entity types found to be highly popular on social media (Ritter et al., 2011). While training examples are obtained by means of distant supervision, our evaluation of MS-NET is conducted using a gold-labeled dataset of entity names extracted from tweets, in which each name string has been annotated with its full set of semantic types. We make this evaluation dataset available to the research community.

To the best of our knowledge, this is the first work to combine diverse information sources, including Web search results, for the purpose of entity name typing. Our results clearly show that the information sources modeled are complimentary—learning using all sources yields the best overall typing performance with respect to both recall and precision. MS-NET improves overall performance compared with a plausible baseline of rule-based alignment to a KB. In particular, a boost in performance is obtained for some of the semantic types evaluated, such as *facility* and *product*, which apply to a long tail of infrequent entity names.

2 Related Work

2.1 Named entity typing

Several recent works have considered a similar problem setting to ours. These works mainly rely on Web-scale lexico-syntactic distributional pro-files of the target name mentions to induce its types.

Lin *et al.* (2012) represent KB-indexed as well as out-of-KB entity names in terms of *subject–relation–object* triplets with which they cooccur in Web documents, extracted using the ReVerb algorithm (Fader et al., 2011). Freebase semantic types are then propagated from indexed to unknown names over common ReVerb triplets. We represent ReVerb distributional patterns as features in our framework. Similarly to previous researchers (Yaghoobzadeh and Schütze, 2015), we find ReVerb triplets to perform poorly when used as a standalone information source. We discuss the reasons for this in detail below.

Yaghoobzadeh and Schütze (2015) presented an embedding based approach for the typing of named entities. They compute embedding vectors for words, entities and semantic types using an annotated version of the ClueWeb Web corpus, in which entity mentions have been tagged with their Freebase IDs. They report poor typing performance for infrequent entity names, possibly because the embedding approach is sensitive to context sparsity (Cui et al., 2015).

In this work, we model distributional lexico-syntactic information within a multi-source learning framework. This distributional information is integrated with knowledge extracted from structured datasets and with global semi-structured contextual signals, obtained via web search. We believe this work to be the first to evaluate named entity typing on twitter messages, which contain relatively many unknown and irregular entity name forms. Our contribution is orthogonal to the works mentioned above, as various types of distributional features can be easily integrated using multi-source learning.

2.2 Semantic type prediction using Web Search

Web search results have been used as an information source for several related semantic tasks. It is a common strategy to enrich Web queries with search results in order to classify them into semantic categories (Shen et al., 2006; Ullegaddi and Varma, 2011). Recently, Web searches have been proven useful for the disambiguation and linking of entities mentioned in search queries to Wikipedia (Carmel et al., 2014; Cornolti et al., 2014). Web queries and micro-blogs are similar to Web queries in that they are short, ambiguous and noisy.

Rüd *et al.* (2011) claim to be first to consider the idea of using search engines as an information source for an NLP problem. They outline a variety of features extracted from search engine results, designed to achieve cross-domain named entity recognition robustness. While their work is evaluated on the classification of Web queries, they conjecture that their approach is similarly applicable to related domains like Twitter and SMS.

This work continues these previous efforts, applying Web search features to the task of named entity typing, and evaluating this task in the social media domain. We find that modeling of global semi-structured contexts obtained via Web search is necessary in order to maintain high cross-domain performance. Unlike previous works, we put emphasis on investigating the synergy between Web search results and other sources of world knowledge, including structured KBs. A detailed evaluation reveals that the best configuration of information sources depends on the characteristics of the target semantic class.

3 Multi-source named entity typing

Let us first formally define the named entity typing task. Given a named entity string e and a set of target semantic types of interest L, our goal is to output a membership function $m : e \times L \mapsto \{0, 1\}$, such that $m(e, \ell)=1$ if e denotes some entity of type $\ell \in L$.[1] The membership relation is not functional, and it is possible that e be associated with any subset of the target types $S \subseteq L$, including the empty set.

We address this multi-class multi-label classification task by learning binary classifiers per label, $C_1, ..., C_{|L|}$, having each classifier C_j predict a binary membership, $m(e, \ell_j) \in (0, 1)$. A main advantage of the binary prediction setting is that it is intuitive, simple, and scalable (Read et al., 2009).

3.1 Knowledge sources

Each name e is represented as a multinomial vector of features, extracted from multiple sources as described below. We illustrate the proposed feature scheme using the running example e='eagles', which maps to the types *sportsteam* and *music artist* according to our annotation.

---

[1]Named entity detection is out of scope of this work. Entity names of interest may be identified automatically (Lin et al., 2012; Hoffart et al., 2014) or manually.

Data: Entity name e, knowledge base k
Result: $S(e)$, a set of semantic types associated with e according to k
initialization;
1. Extract $A(e)$: the set of entities in k, for which e is a possible alias;
2. Initialize $S(e)$;
3. **for** $a \in A(e)$ **do**
  Retrieve S(a): the semantic types of entity a according to k;
  $S(e) = S(e) \cup S(a)$;
end

Algorithm 1: Extraction of semantic types associated with e from a KB

KB tags. Knowledge bases model distinct entities and the relations between them. Typically, entities are associated with a hierarchical structure of semantic types, as well as with lexical aliases (Dalvi et al., 2015). In this work, we extract and represent as features semantic categories associated with the name entity string e in Freebase (FB).

We apply the procedure outlined in Alg. 1 to extract $S^F(e)$, the set of Freebase semantic types associated with the name string e. As described, step (1) of the algorithm involves alignment of the target entity name with possibly matching entities in the KB. In order to increase recall, one can apply proximate string matching in performing this alignment. In this work, we use Freebase API for this purpose, enabling inexact search against known entity aliases.[2] Once relevant entities are identified, their known types are unified to create the set of associated FB types.

47 semantic tags in total were extracted in this fashion for the string 'eagles'. The extracted tags are of high-quality in part, e.g., *sports/professional sports team*, but include also noisy tags, e.g., *base/websites/website*. Noisy tags can be explained by annotation inconsistencies that exist in Freebase, and also result from the proximate alignment of 'eagles' to FB–while increasing recall, proximate matching involves some decrease in precision. In general, databases may include noise also as the result of applying imperfect automatic knowledge population methods.

The set of the KB extracted types has to be mapped to the target type schema L. It is common practice to make use of manually constructed mapping rules to align KB categories against a target semantic schema (Ling and Weld, 2012). We rather apply learning to perform this alignment, having the tags $S^F(e)$ represented as binary fea-

---

[2]We use the filter: "(all name:entity alias:entity)", considering the top three results in the returned ranked hit list. These choices were tuned in preliminary experiments using training examples.

Freebase cateogry tags
fb.base/popstra/topic, fb.base/popstra/sww_base
fb.base/losangelesbands/topic, base/ontologies/ontology_instance
sports/professional_sports_team, base/usnris/nris_listing
base/ovguide/country_musical_groups, base/schemastaging/topic
...
ReVerb patterns
reverbRel.be also a master of
reverbRel.win in
...
Web search features
url.philadelphiaeagles
title.philadelphia.-1, title.official, title.site, title.philadelphia
snippet.philadelphia.-1, snippet.official.1, snippet.team.2
snippet.site.3, snippet.official, snippet.team, snippet.site
snippet.philadelphia, snippet.roster, snippet.new, snippet.history
snippet.youth, snippet.program, snippet.ticket and *snippet.inform*

Table 1: An illustration of the feature types derived from the various sources for $e =$ 'eagles'.

tures, as illustrated in Table 1. Ideally, learning should discard or downweight the features that correspond to irrelevant KB categories.

As discussed above, a main weakness of general knowledge bases as information source is that even large-scale KBs such as Freebase are inherently incomplete. Long tail and emerging entities, as well as informal name forms that are creatively and dynamically used in social media, are likely to be missing or from the KB. In such cases, relevant evidence must be obtained from other sources.

Lexico-syntactic distributional patterns. Named entities and their types may be extracted based on distinctive lexical patterns that surround the target entity mentions (Banko et al., 2007; Carlson et al., 2010).

Distributional semantics may be represented in terms of key phrases (Hoffart et al., 2014), distributional clusters (Roth, 2009), topics (Ritter et al., 2011) or word embeddings (Rong et al., 2016). Similarly to previous works (Lin et al., 2012; Yaghoobzadeh and Schütze, 2015), we consider here lexico-syntactic contexts in the form of *<subject,relation,object>* triplets extracted from Web documents using the ReVerb algorithm (Fader et al., 2011).

We utilize a collection of 15 million ReVerb assertions extracted with high confidence from the ClueWeb09 corpus[3]. Following Lin *et al.* (2012), for each entity name e, we consider the set of assertions in which e appears as subject. The string 'eagles', for example, appears as the subject argument in 140 different patterns in this corpus, including the (lemmatized) triplets *<eagles*, be also a master of, craftsmanship>, and *<eagles*, win in a war of, attrition>. As shown in Table 1, we

---

Figure 1: Top two search results for the query 'eagles'

represent the *relation* argument cooccuring with e as a full string. In preliminary experiments, we also considered a bag-of-word representation of the subject and object arguments, but found those representations to give inferior results.

A manual inspection of the extracted Reverb patterns reveals them to be quite noisy. One reason is ambiguity of the subject argument, which may denote a general noun phrase as well as an entity name. For example, triplets that include *eagles* may refer to mentions of the bird species that the sportsteam is inspired from. As name mentions in social media are often short and ambiguous, they tend to match general noun phrases. Another downside of using distributional statistics as information source is that limited data exists for long tail entity names. Given only a few Web mentions, it is often the case that a long tail name be matched with no Reverb pattern. Finally, as indicated elsewhere (Yaghoobzadeh and Schütze, 2015), these well-formed patterns may not maintain their effectiveness across genres.

Web search results. We wish to further model global Web contexts of the target name e, including the full paragraphs in which it appears, and semi-structured evidence in the form of the Web-page title and source. We obtain this information by means of Web search.

There are several advantages of modeling Web search results that make it appropriate for the processing of social media. Mainly, search engines provide access to nearly real-time raw Web data. They therefore provide good coverage of emerging entities, as well as long tail and noisy name forms that appear frequently on social media.

Having submitted the named entity string as a query to a search engine, we consider the top k retrieved results. Figure 1 shows the top two results for the query 'eagles'. We derive several types of features from these search results.

---

[3] http://reverb.cs.washington.edu/

Given the paragraphs in which e is mentioned ('snippets'), we encode local context information using positional features, denoting the distance and direction of neighboring words within a window of 3 tokens to the right and left of the name mention. These local features are highly specific, and are therefore expected to be sparse. Useful context information can be further derived at paragraph-level (Pritsker et al., 2015)–we therefore additionally represent the whole snippet using count-weighted unigram word features.

We further model the respective Webpage title and source URL, both providing useful semi-structured evidence. Webpage titles are often thematic, and are sometimes generated using wrappers indicative of a source table or list. Likewise, the source URL may map to a domain-specific resource, e.g., *imdb.com* is a Web database that indexes entities in the entertainment domain. We represent titles using positional and bag-of-word features similarly to the snippet. The URL string is split by period and backslash symbols, having each token map to a feature. The full list of generated features per the top search result for 'eagles' are detailed in Table 1.

3.2 Distant learning

As described above, we learn $|L|$ binary classifiers $C_1, ..., C_{|L|}$, having each classifier C_j predict a binary membership $m(x, \ell_j) \in (0, 1)$.

Given labeled examples, a variety of learning methods can be applied to learn C_j. As it is costly to annotate a large set of examples with respect to each category, we adopt a distantly supervised approach. For each target semantic type $\ell \in L$, we obtain relevant entity names from Freebase. Following previous researchers (Ritter et al., 2011; Ling and Weld, 2012), we manually identified Freebase tags that correspond to each category ℓ_j. Entity names were then sampled from the selected Freebase lists, forming a set of positively labeled examples for classifier c_j. In our experiments, we consider a random sample of examples positively associated with the remaining classes, $\ell_i \neq \ell_j$ as negative examples for c_j.

There are several limitations of distant supervision. We expect the distribution of entity names indexed in FB to be different from entity names that are mentioned on social media. In particular, long tail entities are under-represented in Freebase. In addition, the labels obtained using distant supervision may be noisy. (Mainly, negative labels may be false due to FB incompleteness.) Nevertheless, this approach enables one to collect a large number of auto-labeled examples with minimal effort, and is therefore highly adaptive.

4 Experimental setup

For each target type $\ell \in L$, we sampled 900 entity names from relevant Freebase categories. In order to assess and correct possible representation bias, we further sampled 100 additional entity names per category from manually identified Web lists. We found that 18% of the latter names were missing from Freebase. Overall, the constructed training dataset includes about 1,000 unique names per target category. In learning a binary classifier c_j, we uniformly sample an equal number of entity names (1,000) associated with the other classes as negative examples.

We used Google API to perform Web-scale search.[4] Following tuning experiments, in which we examined cross-validation results using the training data, we set the number of top search results modeled per entity name to $k = 15$. We found performance to be relatively insensitive to value of k, as long as at least 5 search results were modeled.

Arguably, search engines inflect bias over the produced rankings. We experimented with shuffling of the top 50 search results (prior to selecting the top 15 results) and found performance to be robust with respect to ranking variance. Furthermore, in our experiments, we ignore exact ranking information, assigning equal importance to each of the selected search results.

We report the results of a strict yet realistic learning setting, in which the classifiers trained using the examples obtained from Freebase and specialized Web lists were applied across domains to a test dataset, which includes entity names found on twitter. We experimented with several classification algorithms using Weka (Hall et al., 2009), and report our results using SVM, which was found to perform best. In the following section we first describe the test dataset, and then turn to discuss the experimental results.

5 Gold labeled evaluation dataset

For evaluation purposes, we manually constructed a gold-labeled dataset of entity names mentioned

---

[4]https://developers.google.com/custom-search

	N	Agreement	Out-of-FB: ratio / examples	
Music artist (MA)	193	0.69	6.2%	*suenalo, shakemode, testing tomorrow*
Company (CO)	155	0.81	6.5%	*indigenous, evergreen Subaru, nex-tech*
Facility (F)	123	0.73	23.6%	*the tall ship silva, belles mansion, knighttime billiards*
Geo location (GL)	245	0.83	2.9%	*robinhoods bay, long island mac Arthur airport, Cromwell field*
Movie (M)	121	0.82	0%	
Product (PR)	141	0.75	11.3%	*Avast AntiVirus 4 8, Air Music Jump, vanilla vodka, Bugatti V*
Sports team (ST)	38	1.00	13.2%	*Marlboro Ducati, Ryerson Quidditch Team, AIS U21, WB Wildcats*
TV show (TV)	70	0.90	2.9%	
Person (P)	356	0.86	8.4%	*denise calaman, Eduardo surita*

Table 2: Statistics of the gold-labeled twitter dataset detailed by semantic type: no. of labels, inter-annotator agreement, and ratio and examples of entity names for which no match in FB was found.

in tweets. We considered a corpus of 2,400 tweets collected by Ritter *et al.* (2011). They have identified the name mentions in this corpus, and annotated these mentions with their contextualized meaning with respect to the following set of types: *music artist, company, facility, geolocation, movie, product, sportsteam, tv-show* and *person*. These types were found to be most popular in the given tweets. A similar set of categories has been used in other works on social media (Gattani et al., 2013; Derczynski et al., 2015).

In order to use this resource for the evaluation of multi-label named entity typing, we have annotated the entity names in the corpus with their full set of types, using the same target category set. Labeling was performed by a graduate student, who was allowed to use any resource available, including Web searches, to determine whether an entity belonged to each of the target classes.

A random subset of 100 entities has been co-annotated by the first author in order to assess inter-agreement rates. Cohen's kappa agreement scores with respect to each of the target classes are detailed in Table 2. As shown, agreement ranges between 0.69–1, denoting substantial to perfect agreement (Landis and Koch, 1977). Interestingly, the lowest agreement was observed for the *music artist* category. We found that disagreements mainly occurred for short, and therefore highly ambiguous, entity names; e.g., 'Justin' may or may not refer to the music artist "justin bieber", and 'MAC' is possibly an alias for "The Mac Band". Somewhat more expectedly, moderate agreement was observed for the *product* and *facility* categories. It is not clear, for example, if 'Twitter' and 'Facebook' are services or products.

The resulting dataset includes 965 distinct entity names and 1,442 label assignments overall. About 27% of the entity names were assigned two classes, and 11% of the entity names were labeled

	P	R	F1	cov.	acc.
FB mapping	*.54*	*.60*	*.57*	*.80*	*.31*
Single-source:					
FB	.53	**.65**	.58	.88	.24
WS: snippet	.53	.60	.56	1.0	.22
WS: title	.46	.59	.52	1.0	.15
WS: URL	.45	**.63**	.53	1.0	.13
WS (all)	**.55**	**.63**	**.59**	1.0	.24
Multi-source:					
WS + FB	**.63**	**.63**	**.63**	1.0	**.32**
WS + RV	**.57**	**.61**	**.59**	1.0	.27
WS + FB + RV	**.65**	**.65**	**.65**	1.0	**.35**

Table 3: Instance-level performance using various information sources and features. Results that improve over the baseline are bold faced.

with three types or more. The corpus includes misspelled, abbreviated, and 'long tail' entity names, such as local restaurants and hotels. Table 2 details the total number, as well as concrete examples, of names per category for which no matching entry was found in Freebase ('Out-of-FB'), despite using a proximate alignment procedure.

This dataset may be first to include gold mappings of entity names into a set of types of interest in the social media domain. We will make the dataset freely available to the research community.

6   Results

Table 3 details our test results on the gold-labeled twitter dataset. We report the following evaluation measures: (i) example-level macro average precision, recall, and F1: these measures are first computed with respect to the set of types assigned to each entity name, and are then averaged over all entity names in the dataset; (ii) coverage: the ratio of entity names for which type predictions were generated. (iii) accuracy: the ratio of names perfectly classified, i.e., having all their types correctly predicted, with no incorrect types assigned to them. The table reports multiple feature configurations, varying the information sources and fea-

Target type	N	FB Mapping			MS-NET			ΔF1
		P	R	F1	P	R	F1	
Music-artist	193	.48	.63	.54	.43	**.69**	.53	*-1.9%*
Company	155	.54	.43	.48	**.61**	**.46**	**.52**	**8.3%**
Facility	123	.46	.33	.38	**.61**	**.55**	**.58**	**52.6%**
Geo-location	245	.69	.72	.70	**.83**	.67	**.74**	**5.7%**
Movie	121	.64	.42	.51	.60	.41	.49	*-3.9%*
Product	141	.49	.40	.44	**.53**	**.50**	**.51**	**15.9%**
Sportsteam	38	.28	.63	.39	**.38**	**.79**	**.51**	**30.8%**
Tv-show	70	.59	.50	.54	.43	**.53**	.47	*-13.0%*
Person	356	.87	.78	.82	.82	.67	.74	*-9.8%*
Macro average		.56	.54	.55	**.58**	**.59**	**.58**	**5.5%**

Table 4: Classifier performance by type. Results that improve over the baseline are bold faced.

Music-artist	Company	Facility
FreebaseType./music/artist	FreebaseType./business/business_operation	snippet.review.0
url.artist	FreebaseType./organization/organization	snippet.locat.0
title.music.0	snippet.compani.0	FreebaseType./architecture/structure
snippet.music.0	url.compani	url.tripadvisor
url.music	FreebaseType./business/employer	FreebaseType./projects/project_focus
snippet.album.0	title.compani.0	FreebaseType./location/location
snippet.song.0	FreebaseType./business/consumer_company	snippet.rate.0
url.fm	url.stock	FreebaseType./architecture/building
title.listen.0	snippet.min.0	url.yelp
title.concert.0	url.invest	url.biz

Geo-location	Movie	Product
FreebaseType./location/location	FreebaseType./film/film	FreebaseType./business/consumer_product
FreebaseType./location/statistical_region	snippet.direct.0	url.product
FreebaseType./location/dated_location	snippet.film.0	url.facebook
FreebaseType./location/citytown	url.titl	snippet.camera.0
snippet.weather.0	snippet.movi.0	title.review.0
title.weather.0	url.imdb	title.facebook.0
snippet.forecast.0	title.imdb.0	snippet.profil.0
snippet.locat.0	title.imdb.2	title.review.1
title.forecast.0	url.movi	snippet.like.0
url.weather	title.movi.0	title.spec.0

Sport-team	Tv-show	Person
FreebaseType./sports/sports_team	FreebaseType./tv/tv_program	FreebaseType./people/person
url.team	title.tv.0	snippet.born.0
snippet.team.0	snippet.episod.0	FreebaseType./people/deceased_person
snippet.club.0	title.tv.1	snippet.born.1
snippet.footbal.0	url.tv	snippet.born.2
FreebaseType./soccer/football_team	title.seri.0	snippet.profession.-2
snippet.leagu.0	snippet.seri.0	snippet.profil.0
title.footbal.0	title.seri.2	snippet.review.0
snippet.fixtur.0	snippet.tv.0	snippet.linkedin.0
snippet.statist.0	snippet.episod.1	url.peopl

Table 5: Top weighted features per category

ture types modeled.

Mapping baseline. As baseline, we consider the plausible strategy of rule-based mapping, aligning $S^F(e)$, the set of Freebase tags extracted for name e (Alg. 1), with the target labels L. We manually determined a set of alignment rules for the purposes of this study, utilizing and expanding rules made previously available by other researchers (Ling and Weld, 2012). As shown, manual mapping applies to 80% of the entity names in the twitter dataset, for which at least one possibly matching entry in Freebase was found. The resulting instance-level precision and recall are .54 and .60. While manual rules tend to be precise, a main source of noise lies in the proximate matching of string e against FB entities. And, hand-picking FB categories for alignment hurts recall.

Single-source learning results. We first discuss our experimental results using each information source separately. Encoding the set of Freebase categories associated with e as features in the learning framework ('FB') substantially improves over the manual alignment rules in terms of coverage (.88 vs. .80) and recall (.65 vs. .60). While both methods use the same resource, the mapping rules rely on fewer high-quality FB categories.

Learning using the features derived from Web search results ('WS') gives perfect coverage. Performance using either snippet, title or URL information is lower compared with the KB-lookup baseline, however when all of the Web search features are modeled, learning outperforms the mapping baseline across all macro-level measures.

Overall, we find that learning using Freebase tags and Web search results as alternative information sources gives comparable performance–instance-level macro-F1 is .58 vs. .59, respectively.

Finally, classification results using ReVerb features ('RV') were poor, and were therefore omitted from the table. The coverage of these features was low, i.e., many of the example entity names were found no matching ReVerb assertions. In addition, as mentioned before, ReVerb patterns are noisy in that they do not distinguish between general noun phrases and named entities. Nevertheless, we found these features to be useful in hybrid configurations, as discussed next.

Multi-source learning. We now review named entity typing results using multi-source learning. The modeling of both Web search and FB features improves on either one of the individual sources, reaching macro-$F1$ performance of .63. As shown, this gain is due to a large improvement in macro-precision, reflected also in higher entity-level accuracy (.32). We thus observe that Web search results and Freebase tags are complimentary in that integrating the two perspectives serves to eliminate noise, while maintaining high recall.

The best-performing system models all of the three information sources ('WS+FB+RV'): macro-precision, recall and $F1$ all measure .65, improving 20.4%, 8.3% and 14% over the mapping baseline, respectively. Similarly, accuracy improves 13% over the baseline. In what follows, we set MS-NET to this best-performing configuration.

Performance by type. Table 4 details the performance of each of the binary classifiers that comprise MS-NET, comparing it against the rule-based mapping baseline. The best results per category are shown in boldface. Table 5 further shows the features with the highest information gain per category.

As shown in Table 4, a boost in performance was achieved using MS-NET for the categories *facility* ($\Delta F1$=52.6%), *sportsteam* (30.8%) and *product* (15.9%). These types apply to a variety of long tail entities, like local restaurants, or amateur sports teams, which are not indexed in Freebase but can be found on the Web (see dataset statistics in Table 2). Moderate performance gains were obtained for the categories *company* (8.3%) and *geolocation* (5.6%).

MS-NET failed to improve on the manual align-ment rules for highly-granular categories like *TV-show* and *movie*. As indicated in Table 2, almost all of the name mentions of these categories in our twitter evaluation dataset are included in Freebase. Automatic imports from external data sources like Wikipedia ensure that FB information in these areas is complete and up-to-date.

Finally, learning failed to improve on person name typing. We found one reason for this to be high ambiguity of person names, resulting sometimes in bias of the search results towards more popular entities with the same name. Consider, for example, the celebrity names *Paris* or *MAC*–in these cases, mentions of the *city* and *product*, respectively, dominate the search results. Sampling of the search results may correct possible bias towards highly popular entities (Anagnostopoulos et al., 2006). Lastly, some of the annotated person names in our dataset refer to non-public figures that have neither KB-, nor Web presence (Gattani et al., 2013).

7   Conclusion

We have presented and evaluated a distantly supervised multi-source learning approach for semantic named entity typing. We believe this work to be the first to model KB information, Web-scale distributional evidence and Web search results as information sources in a joint framework, and the first to evaluate the task of named entity typing in the social media domain.

Our results indicate these various sources to be complimentary–their combination yields best overall performance with respect to both precision and recall. In particular, multi-source learning boosts typing performance for semantic types that apply to out-of-KB entity names, which are prevalent in social media.

One may easily incorporate additional information sources in this general framework–such as additional KBs, lexicons, additional search engines' results, and more elaborate representations of distributional semantics–so as to increase coverage and downweight source-specific bias. Learning-wise, multi-label schemes that model inter-label dependencies may prove useful (Madjarova et al., 2012). Considering the variance in performance across categories, we suggest to identify the best configuration of information sources per target semantic type, possibly using meta-learning.

References

Aris Anagnostopoulos, Andrei Z. Broder, and David Carmel. 2006. Sampling search-engine results. *World Wide Web*, 9(4).

Sören Auer, Christian Bizer, Georgi Kobilarov, Jens Lehmann, and Zachary Ives. 2007. Open information extraction from the web. In *Proceedings of International Joint Conference on Artificial Intelligence (IJCAI)*.

Michele Banko, Michael J. Cafarella, Stephen Soderland, Matt Broadhead, and Oren Etzioni. 2007. Dbpedia: A nucleus for a web of open data. In *Proceedings of International Joint Conference on Artificial Intelligence (IJCAI)*.

Kurt Bollacker, Colin Evans, Praveen Paritosh, Tim Sturge, and Jamie Taylor. 2008. Sfreebase: a collaboratively created graph database for structuring human knowledge. In *Proceedings of the ACM SIGMOD international conference on Management of data (SIGMOD)*.

Antoine Bordes, Jason Weston, and Nicolas Usunier. 2014. Open question answering with weakly supervised embedding models. In *Proceedings of ECML-PKDD*. Springer.

Andrew Carlson, Justin Betteridge, Bryan Kisiel, Burr Settles, Estevam R. Hruschka Jr., and Tom M. Mitchell. 2010. Toward an architecture for never-ending language learning. In *Proceedings of AAAI Conference on Artificial Intelligence (AAAI)*.

David Carmel, Ming-Wei Chang, Evgeniy Gabrilovich, Bo-June (Paul) Hsu, and Kuansan Wang. 2014. Erd'14: Entity recognition and disambiguation challenge. *ACM SIGIR Forum*, 48(2).

Kai-Wei Chang, Wen tau Yih, Bishan Yang, and Christopher Meek. 2014. Typed tensor decomposition of knowledge bases for relation extraction. In *Proceedings of the Conference on Empirical Methods in Natural Language Processing (EMNLP)*.

Marco Cornolti, Paolo Ferragina, Massimiliano Ciaramita, Stefan Rued, and Hinrich Schuetze. 2014. The smaph system for query entity recognition and disambiguation. In *ERD 2014: Entity Recognition and Disambiguation Challenge. SIGIR Forum*.

Qing Cui, Bin Gao, Jiang Bian, Siyu Qiu, Hanjun Dai, and Tie-Yan Liu. 2015. Knet: A general framework for learning word embedding using morphological knowledge. *ACM Transactions on Information Systems (TOIS)*, 34(1).

Bhavana Bharat Dalvi, Einat Minkov, Partha Pratim Talukdar, and William W. Cohen. 2015. Automatic gloss finding for a knowledge base using ontological constraints. In *Proceedings of the ACM International Conference on Web Search and Data Mining (WSDM)*.

Leon Derczynski, Diana Maynard, Giuseppe Rizzo, Marieke van Erp, Genevieve Gorrell, Raphal Troncy, Johann Petrak, and Kalina Bontcheva. 2015. Analysis of named entity recognition and linking for tweets. *Information Processing and Management*, 51:32–49.

Anthony Fader, Stephen Soderland, and Oren Etzioni. 2011. Identifying relations for open information extraction. In *Proceedings of the Conference on Empirical Methods in Natural Language Processing*, EMNLP '11, pages 1535–1545, Stroudsburg, PA, USA. Association for Computational Linguistics.

Yuan Fang and Ming-Wei Chang. 2014. Entity linking on microblogs with spatial and temporal signals. *Transactions of the Association for Computational Linguistics*, 2.

Abhishek Gattani, Digvijay S. Lamba, Nikesh Garera, Mitul Tiwari, Xiaoyong Chai, Sanjib Das, Sri Subramaniam, Arnand Rajaraman, Venky Harinarayan, and AnHai Doan. 2013. Entity extraction, linking, classification, and tagging for social media: a wikipedia-based approach. *Proceedings of the VLDB Endowment*, 6(11):1126–1137.

Mark Hall, Eibe Frank, Geoffrey Holmes, Bernhard Pfahringer, Peter Reutemann, and Ian H. Witten. 2009. The weka data mining software: An update. *SIGKDD Explorations*, 11(1).

Johannes Hoffart, Yasemin Altun, and Gerhard Weikum. 2014. Discovering emerging entities with ambiguous names. In *23rd International World Wide Web Conference, WWW '14, Seoul, Republic of Korea, April 7-11, 2014*, pages 385–396.

J. Richard Landis and Gary G. Koch. 1977. The measurement of observer agreement for categorical data. *Biometrics*, 33(1):159–174.

Thomas Lin, Mausam, and Oren Etzioni. 2012. No noun phrase left behind: Detecting and typing unlinkable entities. In *Proceedings of the Conference on Empirical Methods in Natural Language Processing and Computational Natural Language Learning (EMNLP-CONLL)*.

Xiao Ling and Daniel S. Weld. 2012. Fine-grained entity recognition. In *Proceedings of the 26th Conference on Artificial Intelligence (AAAI)*.

Gjorgji Madjarova, Dragi Kocevb, Dejan Gjorgjevikja, and Sašo Džeroskib. 2012. An extensive experimental comparison of methods for multi-label learning. *Pattern Recognition*, 45(9).

Marius Pasca. 2004. Acquisition of categorized named entities for web search. In *Proceedings of the ACM International Conference on Information and Knowledge Management (CIKM)*.

Evgenia Wasserman Pritsker, William W. Cohen, and Einat Minkov. 2015. Learning to identify the best contexts for knowledge-based wsd. In *Proceedings of the Conference on Empirical Methods in Natural Language Processing (EMNLP)*.

Jesse Read, Bernhard Pfahringer, Geoff Holmes, and Eibe Frank. 2009. Classifier chains for multi-label classification. In W. Buntine, M. Grobelnik, D. Mladenic, and J. Shawe-Taylor, editors, *Lecture Notes in Artificial Intelligence*. Springer.

Alan Ritter, Sam Clark, Mausam, and Oren Etzioni. 2011. Named entity recognition in tweets: an experimental study. In *EMNLP*.

Xin Rong, Zhe Chen, Qiaozhu Mei, and Eytan Adar. 2016. Egoset: Exploiting word ego-networks and user-generated ontology for multifaceted set expansion. In *ACM International Conference on Web Search and Data Mining (WSDM)*.

Lev Ratinov Dan Roth. 2009. Design challenges and misconceptions in named entity recognition. In *Proceedings of the Conference on Computational Natural Language Learning (CoNLL)*.

Stefan Rüd, Massimiliano Ciaramita, Jens Müller, and Hinrich Schütze. 2011. Piggyback: using search engines for robust cross-domain named entity recognition. In *Proceedings of the 49th Annual Meeting of the Association for Computational Linguistics (ACL)*.

Dou Shen, Jian-Tao Sun, Qiang Yang, and Zheng Chen. 2006. Building bridges for web query classification. In *Proceedings of the annual international ACM SIGIR conference on Research and development in information retrieval (SIGIR)*.

Fabian M. Suchanek, Gjergji Kasneci, and Gerhard Weikum. 2007. Yago: A core of semantic knowledge unifying wordnet and wikipedia. In *Proceedings of the International World Wide Web Conference (WWW)*.

Prashant Ullegaddi and Vasudeva Varma. 2011. Learning to rank categories for web queries. In *Proceedings of the ACM International Conference on Information and Knowledge Management (CIKM)*.

Chi Wang, Kaushik Chakrabarti, Tao Cheng, and Surajit Chaudhuri. 2012. Targeted disambiguation of ad-hoc, homogeneous sets of named entities. In *Proceedings of the International World Wide Web Conference (WWW)*.

Robert West, Evgeniy Gabrilovich Kevin Murphy, Shaohua Sun, Rahul Gupta, and Dekang Lin. 2014. Knowledge base completion via search-based question answering. In *Proceedings of the international conference on World wide web (WWW)*.

Yadollah Yaghoobzadeh and Hinrich Schütze. 2015. Corpus-level fine-grained entity typing using contextual information. In *Proceedings of the Conference on Empirical Methods in Natural Language Processing (EMNLP)*.

Ikuya Yamada, Hideaki Takeda, and Yoshiyasu Takefuji. 2015. Enhancing named entity recognition in messages using entity linking. In *Proceedings of the ACL 2015 Workshop on Noisy User-generated Text*.

Xuchen Yao and Benjamin Van Durme. 2014. Information extraction over structured data: Question answering with freebase. In *Proceedings of the 52nd Annual Meeting of the Association for Computational Linguistics (ACL)*.

Evaluating and Combining Named Entity Recognition Systems

Ridong Jiang
Institute for Infocomm
Research, A*STAR
Singapore 138632
`rjiang@i2r.a-star.edu.sg`

Rafael E. Banchs
Institute for Infocomm
Research, A*STAR
Singapore 138632
`rembanchs@i2r.a-star.edu.sg`

Haizhou Li
Institute for Infocomm
Research, A*STAR
Singapore 138632
`hli@i2r.a-star.edu.sg`

Abstract

Name entity recognition (NER) is an important subtask in natural language processing. Various NER systems have been developed in the last decade. They may target for different domains, employ different methodologies, work on different languages, detect different types of entities, and support different inputs and output formats. These conditions make it difficult for a user to select the right NER tools for a specific task. Motivated by the need of NER tools in our research work, we select several publicly available and well-established NER tools to validate their outputs against both Wikipedia gold standard corpus and a small set of manually annotated documents. All the evaluations show consistent results on the selected tools. Finally, we constructed a hybrid NER tool by combining the best performing tools for the domains of our interest.

1 Introduction

Name entity recognition is an important subtask in natural language processing (NLP). The results of recognition and classification of proper nouns in a text document are widely used in information retrieval, information extraction, machine translation, question answering and automatic summarization (Nadeau and Sekine. 2007; Kaur and Gupta. 2010). Depending on the requirements of specific tasks, the types to be recognized can be person, location, organization and date, which are mostly used in newswire (Tjong et al., 2003), or other commonly used measures (percent, weight, money), email address, etc. It can also be domain specific entity types such as medical drug names, disease symptoms and treatment, etc. (Asma Ben Abacha and Pierre Zweigenbaum, 2001).

Name entity recognition is a challenging task which needs massive prior knowledge sources for better performance (Lev Ratinov, Dan Roth, 2009; Nadeau and Sekine. 2007). Many researches works have been conducted in different domains with various approaches. Early studies focus on heuristic and handcrafted rules. By defining the formation patterns and context over lexical-syntactic features and term constituents, entities are recognized by matching the patterns against the input documents (Rau, Lisa F. 1991; Collins, Michael, Singer, Y. 1999). Rule-based system may achieve high degree of precision. However, the development process is time-consuming and porting these developed rules from one domain to another is a major challenge. Recent research in NER tends to use machine learning approaches (Andrew Borthwick. 1999; McCallum, Andrew and Li, W. 2003; Takeuchi K. and Collier N. 2002). The learning methods include various supervised, semi-supervised and unsupervised learning. The supervised learning tends to be the dominant technique for named entity recognition and classification (David Nadeau and Satoshi Sekine. 2007). However, supervised machine learning methods require large amount of annotated documents for model training and its performance typically depends on the availability of sufficient high quality training data in the domain of interest. There are some systems which use hybrid methods to combine different rule-based and/or machine learning systems for improved performance over individual

Proceedings of the Sixth Named Entity Workshop, joint with 54th ACL, pages 21–27,
Berlin, Germany, August 12, 2016. ©2016 Association for Computational Linguistics

approaches (Srihari R. et al., 2000; Tim R. et al., 2012). Hybrid systems make the best use of the good features of different systems or methods to achieve the best overall performance.

In this paper, we first select several publicly available and well-established NER tools in section 2. Then all the tools are validated in section 3 with CONLL 2003 metrics and a customized partial matching measurement. Then we constructed a hybrid NER system based on the best performed NER tools in section 4.

2 Methodology

2.1 Tool Selection

Our goal is to evaluate freely available NER tools that have good performance for our research projects. The criteria for our selection are as follows:

a) The NER tool is freely available and allows unlimited use.
b) The tool can be downloaded and installed locally and works well with default configuration.
c) The tool is not trained for a specific domain.
d) The tool must be able to recognize the basic three entity types: PERSON, LOCATION, ORGANIZATION

Based on the above criteria, the following NER tools have been selected:

a) Stanford NER (Jenny Rose Finkel et al., 2005).
b) spaCy[1].
c) Alias-i LingPipe (Alias-i. 2008).
d) Natural Language Toolkit (NLTK) (Bird Steven et al. 2009).

2.2 Normalization

The selected tools come with different features, programming languages as well as different tag set and output format. To have an automated and efficient evaluation system, we have to integrate all these tools in one system and normalize all their outputs into a standard format.

Stanford NER is a Java package (version 3.6.0). It is based on linear chain Conditional Random Field (Jenny Rose Finkel et al., 2005). The models were trained on a mixture of CoNLL, MUC-6, MUC-7 and ACE named entity corpora. The basic required output tags are "PERSON", "LOCATION" and "ORGANIZATION".

spaCy is implementation in Python. There is no detailed information provided in its documentation with regard to its implemented models at the time of writing. The related output tags include "PERSON", "LOC", "ORG", "GPE" etc. For spaCy outputs, we map "LOC" to "LOCATION", "ORG" and "GPE" to "ORGANIZATION" and ignore all other types.

Alias-i LingPipe NER is implemented in Java and supports both rule-based NER and supervised training of a statistical model or more direct method like dictionary matching (Alias-i. 2008). We use version 4.1.0 and adopt the "First-best Named Entity Chunking". The trained model is News English on the MUC 6 corpus which is relatively slow compared with its other models but with higher accuracy. The output entity types match the normalized types and no mapping is needed.

NLTK is a python NLP toolkit and is well-established in the research community. NLTK's named entity chunker is based on a supervised machine learning algorithm – Maximum Entropy Classifier. Its model is trained on ACE corpus with the exact entity types which we are interested in: "PERSON", "LOCATION" and "ORGANIZATION". It also outputs "GPE" type which we will map to "LOCATION" for evaluation.

2.3 Integration

In order to automate the evaluation process, we developed a system to integrate all the toolkits into one system using a python script.

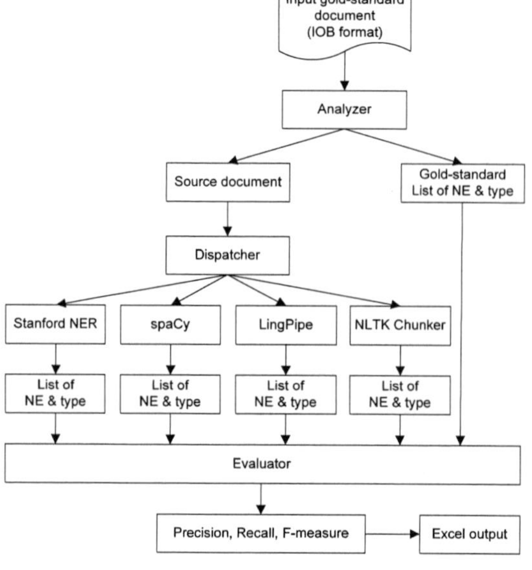

---

[1] https://spacy.io/

Fig. 1. System diagram for automated evaluation

The overall system structure of the integrated evaluation system is shown in Fig. 1.

In the process of evaluation, an annotated (gold-standard) input document must be provided. Currently, the supported format is IOB (short for Inside, Outside, Beginning) (Ramshaw and Marcus, 1995). In this scheme, every line in the file represents one token with two fields: the word itself and its named entity type. Empty lines denote sentence boundaries. Following is an example of the representation:

Albert I-PERSON
Einstein I-PERSON
was O
born O
in O
Ulm I-LOCATION
. O

The prefix "I-" in the tag means that the tag is inside a chunk. While the prefix "B-" indicates that the tag is the beginning of a chunk and is only used when a tag is followed by a tag of the same type without "O" tag between them. The "O" tag just means it is out of the chunk. This IOB chunk representation is much easier for manual annotation than inside XML annotation scheme.

An Analyzer module is used to extract the source document as well as all chunks and their types from the annotated file. Every chunk is represented in the format of a three-element tuple: (*chunk, type, start_position*), where the *start_position* is the sequence position (character index) of the chunk in the source document. This tuple representation contains all the necessary information for the validation of a chunk, including its boundary.

The Dispatcher module will pass the source document to all NER tools. All the tools will first tokenize the sentences, analyze these sentences and then create their respective list of tuples dynamically. Every output list from the NER tools will be compared against the standard list generated from the annotated file. The comparison results will be used to calculate true positives (TP), false positives (FP) and false negatives (FN). Then precision, recall and F-measure can be further calculated for evaluation. All the calculation results can be directly exported to excel file for easy comparison.

3 Evaluation

With the methodology defined in section 2, it is ready to evaluate all the selected tools with any data file annotated in the IOB format.

3.1 Evaluation Corpus

Since all the selected NER tools are able to classify the three entity types: PERSON, LOCATION and ORGANIZATION, the evaluation corpus must contain at least the above three entity types. The format is better to be in the supported IOB chunk representation. We found that WikiGold [2] meets the above requirements. WikiGold (Balasuriya et al. 2009) is an annotated corpus over a small sample of Wikipedia articles in CoNLL format (IOB). It contains 145 documents (separated by "-DOCSTART-"), 1696 sentences and 39152 tokens. The statistics of named entities is shown in table 1.

Entity Type	PER	LOC	ORG	MISC	Total
No.	931	1014	898	712	3555

Table 1. WikiGold entities

In the evaluation, we ignore the MISC type and map the gold standard types: PER, LOC and ORG to normalized types PERSON, LOCATION and ORGANIZATION respectively.

3.2 Evaluation Metrics

There are different evaluation metrics for the evaluation of NER systems (Nadeau and Sekine. 2007). The evaluation is basically to check the tool's ability on finding the boundaries of names and their correct types. Most evaluation systems require exact match on both boundary and entity type. The share task for CONLL 2003 (Sang and Meulder, 2003) is one of the examples for the exact matching. However, in some cases, the exact boundary detection is not so important as long as the major part of the name has been identified. For instance, "The United Nations" and "United Nations", "in November 2015" and "November 2015", they are almost the same except the minor differences in the definite article and preposition. The metrics used for evaluation in the Message Understanding

---

[2] http://downloads.schwa.org/wikiner/wikigold.conll.txt

Conference (MUC) (Grishman and Sundheim, 1996) adopted more loose matching conditions which allow for partial credit when partial span or wrong type detection happened. The credit was given to any correct entity type detected regardless of its boundary as long as there is an overlap, as well as the correct boundary identified regardless of the type. Here we score NER systems based on the following two metrics:

a) Exact matching for both boundary and type (similar to CONLL) which measures a system's capability for accurate named entity detection.

b) Partial matching for boundary is also counted, only when the detected type is correct. This measurement will mitigate the failures of exact matching when the boundary differences are caused by some unimportant words in the names such as the articles and prepositions.

Based on the above two scoring protocols, the measuring system counts TP, FP and FN for every NER toolkit. Then typical precision: $p = TP / (TP + FP)$ and recall: $R = TP / (TP + FN)$ are further calculated to check the NER system's type I (false alarm) and type II (miss) errors respectively.

3.3 Results

		PER	LOC	ORG	OVERALL
Stanford	P	0.7195	0.7753	0.6992	0.7359
	R	0.8733	0.7416	0.4143	0.6813
	F	0.7890	0.7581	0.5203	0.7075
	PP	0.7496	0.8309	0.8083	0.7914
	PR	0.9098	0.7949	0.4788	0.7327
	PF	0.8220	0.8125	0.6014	0.7609
spaCy	P	0.7286	0.7321	0.3346	0.6110
	R	0.7325	0.6144	0.2873	0.5498
	F	0.7305	0.6681	0.3092	0.5788
	PP	0.7788	0.8085	0.5642	0.7240
	PR	0.7830	0.6785	0.4844	0.6514
	PF	0.7809	0.7378	0.5213	0.6858
LingPipe	P	0.4840	0.5067	0.2425	0.4026
	R	0.4211	0.4822	0.2806	0.3985
	F	0.4504	0.4941	0.2602	0.4005
	PP	0.6025	0.6052	0.4341	0.5412
	PR	0.5242	0.5759	0.5022	0.5357
	PF	0.5606	0.5902	0.4657	0.5384
NLTK	P	0.4802	0.4463	0.3115	0.4228
	R	0.7164	0.5493	0.3396	0.5378
	F	0.5750	0.4925	0.3249	0.4734
	PP	0.5587	0.4832	0.4883	0.5136
	PR	0.8335	0.5947	0.5323	0.6532
	PF	0.6690	0.5332	0.5094	0.5750

Table 2. Evaluation results on the WikiGold annotated data for the selected NER tools

Table 2 shows the results of the four selected NER systems on the WikiGold data set.

In the table, Precision (P), Recall (R) and F1 measure (F) are calculated against every entity type and a final overall score is also given for all the measurements. Similarly, the Precision (PP), Recall (PR) and F1 measure (PF) for partial boundary matching as described in section 3.2 are also calculated. From the results depicted in Table 2 we can derive the following conclusions:

a) Loose boundary matching shows better results than the exact matching for every entity type across all the NER tools. That means there exist quite a number of cases where NER systems detected the right entity types but the boundaries are not exactly matched.

b) ORGANIZATION appears to be the entity type which is more difficult for detecting for all the NER tools. This is proved by its lower scores compared with the PERSON and LOCATION types.

c) Stanford NER and spaCy generally show better performance in this data set for both exact matching and partial matching.

4 Configuration of Hybrid NER System

4.1 Hybrid NER System

We need to have a NER system which is able to recognize PERSON, LOCATION, ORGANIZATION as well as DATE for our research projects. Among the evaluated NER tools, we selected the Stanford NER and spaCy for the configuration of the proposed hybrid NER system. Both tools showed good scores in our previous evaluation and are able to identify DATE entity without any extra setting (Stanford NER 7-class model includes the DATE type).

Our first target domain of application is Wikipedia pages about Singapore. To construct the hybrid NER system, we simply combined the outputs of the Stanford NER system and spaCy NER by using union method. In addition, a dictionary with limited entries on PERSON, LOCATION and ORGANIZATION about Singapore was also created with the expectation of improving system precision (Tsuruoka and Tsujii 2003; Cohen and Sarawagi, 2004). We set the dictionary to have the highest priority when there is any conflict with the outputs from other tools. Then followed by Stanford NER tool, it has the second highest priority on the determination of final named entities.

4.2 Data for Evaluation

In order to evaluate the performance of the hybrid system, we manually annotated twenty two web pages. All the web pages are from Singapore National Library Board eResources[3]. Half of the web pages are about Singapore history, another half are from Infopedia pages. We first use Stanford tool to tokenize all the documents and save them into different files. Every token is in a new line with a space line to separate the sentence. Then every token is manually annotated in IOB format. Table 3 shows the statistics of the two manually annotated datasets.

Entity Type	PER	LOC	ORG	DATE	Total
History	108	158	103	161	530
Infopedia	94	158	121	250	623

Table 3. Entity statistics on History and Infopedia testing datasets

When applying the same evaluation metrics as defined in section 3.2, we have the results on History data and Infopedia data as shown in table 4 and 5 respectively.

		PER	LOC	ORG	DATE	OVER ALL
Stanford	P	0.8649	0.8759	0.7527	0.7000	0.8004
	R	0.8889	0.7595	0.6796	0.5652	0.7113
	F	0.8767	0.8136	0.7143	0.6254	0.7532
	PP	0.8829	0.9270	0.8065	1.0000	0.9130
	PR	0.9074	0.8038	0.7282	0.8075	0.8113
	PF	0.8950	0.8610	0.7654	0.8935	0.8592
spaCy	P	0.7500	0.7889	0.3303	0.7407	0.6479
	R	0.6389	0.4494	0.3495	0.6211	0.5208
	F	0.6900	0.5726	0.3396	0.6756	0.5774
	PP	0.9022	0.9000	0.6055	0.9704	0.8474
	PR	0.7685	0.5127	0.6408	0.8137	0.6811
	PF	0.8300	0.6533	0.6227	0.8852	0.7552
Hybrid	P	0.8673	0.8212	0.7203	0.7962	0.8015
	R	0.9074	0.7848	0.8252	0.7764	0.8151
	F	0.8869	0.8026	0.7692	0.7862	0.8082
	PP	0.8761	0.8874	0.7458	0.9809	0.8813
	PR	0.9167	0.8481	0.8544	0.9565	0.8962
	PF	0.8959	0.8673	0.7964	0.9685	0.8887

---

[3] http://eresources.nlb.gov.sg/index.aspx

Table 4. Evaluation results on History testing dataset

		PER	LOC	ORG	DATE	OVER ALL
Stanford	P	0.8500	0.8701	0.7080	0.7208	0.7819
	R	0.9043	0.8481	0.6612	0.5680	0.7079
	F	0.8763	0.8590	0.6838	0.6353	0.7431
	PP	0.8700	0.9091	0.7699	1.0000	0.9060
	PR	0.9255	0.8861	0.7190	0.7880	0.8202
	PF	0.8969	0.8975	0.7436	0.8814	0.8610
spaCy	P	0.6095	0.8917	0.2846	0.8551	0.6901
	R	0.6809	0.6772	0.2893	0.7080	0.6148
	F	0.6432	0.7698	0.2869	0.7746	0.6503
	PP	0.6952	0.9250	0.5610	1.0000	0.8288
	PR	0.7766	0.7025	0.5702	0.8280	0.7384
	PF	0.7336	0.7985	0.5656	0.9059	0.7810
Hybrid	P	0.7179	0.8187	0.5706	0.8826	0.7636
	R	0.8936	0.8861	0.7686	0.8120	0.8347
	F	0.7962	0.8511	0.6550	0.8458	0.7976
	PP	0.7436	0.8889	0.6196	1.0000	0.8370
	PR	0.9255	0.9620	0.8347	0.9200	0.9149
	PF	0.8246	0.9240	0.7112	0.9583	0.8742

Table 5. Evaluation results on Infopedia testing dataset

From the evaluation results on the History and Infopedia datasets, we can have the following remarks:

a) All the conclusions we drew from evaluation results over WikiGold dataset are still valid for the two manually annotated datasets: History and Infopedia.

b) Stanford NER generally shows good performance on all tested datasets. However, its scores on DATE entity type are not as good as spaCy. After further analysis on the false alarm and missing errors, we noticed that Stanford NER has difficulty to identify the full date information from the text. For instance, from text *"on 1 February 1858"*, it can only identify *"February 1858"*, the date is always missing. This problem is probably caused by the fact that Stanford NER is not trained for the date format "date month year". An alternative solution is to use its rule-based Temporal Tagger (SUTime). However, this is not included in the current evaluation.

c) The hybrid system usually has lower precision and higher recall than Stanford NER for entity types: PERSON, LOCATION, and ORGANIZATION. Its F1-measure is slightly better than Stanford

NER for History data for these three entity types, but slight worse for Infopedia data.

d) In general, the hybrid system has better overall performance over both Stanford NER and spaCy. This is especially true for History testing data. However, most of the advantages are contributed by its better DATE entity recognition.

e) Overall, all the NER tools, including the hybrid system, showed better performance on History data than Infopedia data. This is mostly caused by some noise present in the Infopedia documents, for instance, html codes: *’*, un-delimited words *"COMPASS.FamilyWife"* in the document due to the data extraction from the html pages.

5   Related Work

Different NER systems have been developed in the community and a number of them are freely available in the form of downloadable source codes/executables, web services or application programming interface for research purpose or limited use. Although these NER tools may differ in targeting domains, supported languages, processing methodologies, recognized entity types, and input/output formats, they can be evaluated in one way or another by applying the same evaluation metrics, such as traditional precision and recall. Marrero et al. (2009) evaluated ten NER tools which are targeting for general domains and English language. A small test corpus containing 579 English words are used for validation and observed that the variety of entity types that the tools can recognize does not determine the results. Atdag and Labatut (2013) compared four NER tools which include Stanford NER, Illinois NET, OpenCalais NER WS and Alias-i LingPipe for biographical texts. They created and annotated a new corpus from 247 Wikipedia articles and assessed their performance. They concluded that the testing results show a clear hierarchy between the tested tools: first Stanford NER, then LingPipe, Illinois NET and finally OpenCalais. Their results agree with our testing results for the two selected common NER tools. Kepa et al. 2012 evaluated the efficacy of four NER tools (OpenNLP, Stanford NER, AlchemyAP and OpenCalais) at extracting entities directly from the output of an optical character recognition (OCR) workflow. Their experiments showed that Stanford NER gave overall the best performance across two datasets, and was most effective on PER and LOC types. Alchemy API achieved the best results for the ORG type. In this paper, our work is different from the above mentioned validation tasks in the following ways:

a) We developed a validation framework which can work with various NER tools regardless of their programming languages. All the tools can work dynamically for immediate validation against gold standard corpus. The comparing results can be presented in text document or directly exported to excel file in predefined table format.

b) The selected tools are evaluated with both publicly available gold standard corpus and our manually annotated datasets.

c) After evaluating the selected NER tools, a further step was taken by combining the best performing NER tools in an effort to construct a new hybrid NER tool for our application domain.

6   Conclusion

In this paper, we conducted a comparative evaluation of four publically available and well-established NER tools which include Stanford NER, spaCy, Alias-i LingPipe and NLTK. For validation purposes, a framework has been developed in python, which can seamlessly work with different NER systems implemented in different programming languages. The output can be produced dynamically in both text documents or excel tables. The selected NER tools were evaluated by using publicly available gold standard corpus and our manually annotated datasets. Results showed that Stanford NER, followed by spaCy, performed the best across all the testing datasets. We further constructed a hybrid NER tool for our application domain by combining the best two performing NER tools.

In the future, we plan to continue improving the overall performance of the hybrid NER system by combining different features of more advanced systems as well as rule-based components.

Acknowledgements

We would like to thank Singapore National Library Board for providing all the original documents for our testing and validation.

Reference

David Nadeau and Satoshi Sekine. 2007. A survey of named entity recognition and classification. *Journal of Linguisticae Investigationes*, 30:3-26.

Darvinder Kaur, Vishal Gupta. 2010. A survey of Name Entity Recognition in English and other Indian Langauges. *IJCSI International Journal of Computer Science,* Issues, Vol. 7, Issue 6.

Tjong Kim Sang, Erik. F., De Meulder, F. 2003. Introduction to the CoNLL-2003 Shared Task: Language-Independent Named Entity Recognition. In *Proc. Conference on Natural Language Learning.* pp. 142-147. Edmonton, Canada (2003).

Asma Ben Abacha, Pierre Zweigenbaum, 2001, Medical Entity Recognition: A Comparison of Semantic and Statistical Methods. *Proceedings of the 2011 Workshop on Biomedical Natural Language Processing*, ACL-HLT 2011, pages 56–64, Portland, Oregon, USA, June 23-24.

Lev Ratinov, Dan Roth, 2009. Design Challenges and Misconceptions in Named Entity Recognition, *Proceedings of the Thirteenth Conference on Computational Natural Language Learning (CoNLL)*, pages 147–155, Boulder, Colorado, June 2009.

Rau, Lisa F. 1991. Extracting Company Names from Text. *In Proc. Conference on Artificial Intelligence Applications of IEEE.*

Collins, Michael; Singer, Y. 1999. Unsupervised Models for Named Entity Classification. *In Proc. of the Joint SIGDAT Conference on Empirical Methods in Natural Language Processing and Very Large Corpora.*

Andrew Borthwick. 1999. Maximum Entropy Approach to Named Entity Recognition, *Ph.D. thesis, New York University.*

McCallum, Andrew; Li, W. 2003. Early Results for Named Entity Recognition with Conditional Random Fields, Features Induction and Web-Enhanced Lexicons. *In Proc. Conference on Computational Natural Language Learning.*

Takeuchi K. and Collier N. 2002. Use of Support Vector Machines in extended named entity recognition, *in the proceedings of the sixth Conference on Natural Language Learning (CoNLL-2002)*, Taipei, Taiwan

Tim Rocktäschel, Michael Weidlich and Ulf Leser, 2012. ChemSpot: a hybrid system for chemical named entity recognition. *Bioinformatics* 2012; 28:1633-40.

Srihari R., Niu C. and Li W. 2000. A Hybrid Approach for Named Entity and Sub-Type Tagging, *in the proceedings of the sixth Conference on Applied Natural Language Processing.*

Jenny Rose Finkel, Trond Grenager, and Christopher Manning. 2005. Incorporating Non-local Information into Information Extraction Systems by Gibbs Sampling. *Proceedings of the 43nd Annual Meeting of the Association for Computational Linguistics (ACL 2005),* pp. 363-370.

Alias-i. 2008. LingPipe 4.1.0. *http://alias-i.com/lingpipe* (accessed October 1, 2008).

Bird Steven, Ewan Klein, and Edward Loper, 2009. Natural Language, Processing with Python, *O'Reilly Media.*

Lance A. Ramshaw and Mitchell P. Marcus. 1995. Text Chunking Using Transformation-Based Learning. *In Proceedings of the Third ACL Workshop on Very Large Corpora*, pages 82–94. Cambridge, MA, USA.

Dominic Balasuriya, Nicky Ringland, Joel Nothman, Tara Murphy, James R. Curran, 2009. Named Entity Recognition inWikipedia, Proceedings of the 2009 Workshop on the People's Web Meets NLP, ACL-IJCNLP 2009, pages 10–18.

Grishman, Ralph and Sundheim, B. 1996. Message Understanding Conference - 6: A Brief History. *In Proc. International Conference on Computational Linguistics.*

Tsuruoka, Yoshimasa and Tsujii, J. 2003. Boosting Precision and Recall of Dictionary-Based Protein Name Recognition. *In Proc. Conference of Association for Computational Linguistics. Natural Language Processing in Biomedicine.*

Cohen, William W., Sarawagi, S. 2004. Exploiting Dictionaries in Named Entity Extraction: Combining Semi-Markov Extraction Processes and Data Integration Methods. *In Proc. Conference on Knowledge Discovery in Data.*

M. Marrero, S. Sanchez-Cuadrado, J. Lara, and G. Andreadakis. 2009. Evaluation of Named Entity Extraction Systems. *Advances in Computational Linguistics, Research in Computing Science*, 41:47–58.

S. Atdag and V. Labatut, 2013. A Comparison of Named Entity Recognition Tools Applied to Biographical Texts. *CoRR abs/1308.0661*, 2013.

Kepa Joseba Rodriquez, Mike Bryant, Tobias Blanke, Magdalena Luszczynska, 2012. Comparison of Named Entity Recognition tools for raw OCR text, *Proceedings of KONVENS 2012* (LThist 2012 workshop), Vienna, September 21, 2012.

German NER with a Multilingual Rule Based Information Extraction System: Analysis and Issues

Anna Druzhkina
National Research University
Higher School of Economics;
ABBYY
annarya@gmail.com

Alexey Leontyev
ABBYY
Aleksey_L@abbyy.com

Maria Stepanova
ABBYY
Maria_Ste@abbyy.com

Abstract

This paper presents a rule-based approach to Named Entity Recognition for the German language. The approach rests upon deep linguistic parsing and has already been applied to English and Russian. In this paper we present the first results of our system, ABBYY InfoExtractor, on GermEval 2014 Shared Task corpus. We focus on the main challenges of German NER that we have encountered when adapting our system to German and possible solutions for them.

1 Introduction

Named Entity Recognition (NER), which is a sub-task of information extraction (Grishman, 2003), is a well-studied, yet challenging task. Various competitions have been held to evaluate quality of named entity recognition for different languages (MUC, CONLL-2002, IREX). German is no exception: there have already been two evaluation tracks for German, ConLL 2003 (Tjong Kim Sang and De Meulder, 2003) and GermEval 2014 (Benikova et al., 2014). The best results reported for the tracks are 72.41% and 76.38% respectively, which is still considerably below the results for English. One of the observed reasons is that noun capitalization in German differs considerably from that in English. Another reason is the smaller number of gazetteers and other linguistic resources available for German. In this paper we present an overview of our approach to Named Entity Recognition and discuss the issues that we have observed while adapting our information extraction system to German.

ABBYY InfoExtractor has already been applied to English and Russian. We evaluated our named entity recognition system for English on MUC-6 corpus and achieved the F-measure of approximately 83% with no prior adjustments. We performed this evaluation ourselves. As for the Russian language, we took part in FactRuEval 2016 competition[1] and showed the best results in the Russian Named Entity Recognition Track with the F-measure of 86.7% (Stepanova et al., 2016; Starostin et al., 2016).

The paper is structured as follows. In Section 2 we review some of the previous works in the field of German NER. In Section 3 an outline of the system architecture is given. In Section 4 we discuss the issues that we have faced in German NER and comment on them. In Section 5 we present performance of our system on GermEval 2014 corpus. Section 6 provides conclusion and discussion of our future work.

2 Related Work

There have been two main approaches to named entity recognition: rule-based and classifier-based. Most of the systems that work with the German language are classifier-based: only four of the systems that took part in either GermEval 2014 or CONLL 2003 tracks used handcrafted rules for named entity recognition (Bobkova et al., 2014; Hermann et al., 2014; Weber and Pötzl, 2014; Watrin et al., 2014), three of these systems used rules in combination with classifier-based approaches. Hatner (2014) reports that the combination of rules and a classifier performed actually worse than the classifier alone. However, Early-

---

[1] http://www.dialog-21.ru/en/evaluation/

Proceedings of the Sixth Named Entity Workshop, joint with 54th ACL, pages 28–33,
Berlin, Germany, August 12, 2016. ©2016 Association for Computational Linguistics

Tracks reported that the use of linguistic resources and rules improved the resulting F-measure considerably. NERU was the only system which relied mainly on handcrafted rules, the system was able to achieve the F-measure of 54.55% on the test set. Overall, the systems participating in GermEval track showed F-measures from 37.23% to 76.38%.

3 System Architecture

Our approach rests upon deep linguistic parsing performed by ABBYY Compreno parser. The input of information extraction module is semantic and syntactic structures of text produced by the parser.

3.1 Language model

The language model we use can be described as projective dependency trees. Alternatively, it can be viewed as flat constituent structures where every constituent is built around a word. Dependency arcs have two types of labels, syntactic and semantic ones. Syntactically, our structures are very similar to universal dependency model (Nivre, 2015). Semantic labels include traditional semantic roles (Agent, Instrument, Object, Time etc.) as well as several 'dummy' labels (such as Specification) devoid of semantic content.

Leaves of dependency trees are mostly word forms annotated with lexeme and lexical meaning (similar in spirit to WordNet (Fellbaum, 1998) meanings). Quoted expressions, e.g. "'War and Peace' is a masterpiece", have their own dummy nodes as well. The system is designed as multilingual, which is manifested as follows. Lexical meanings in a given language are leaves in a language-independent hierarchy of meanings. Semantic labels are universal for all languages as well. Syntactic structures across different languages are aligned as much as possible.

The pipeline of the system consists of the following steps. Input text undergoes lexical and morphological analysis, at which stage all possible lexical classes for each word form with all possible grammatical values are suggested. At the next step the syntactic module builds a graph of all possible syntactic and semantic dependencies between the lemmas. At the same time non-tree relations, if any, are checked. Incompatible meanings are gradually filtered, and a set of valid syntactic-semantic trees remains. Then the tree with the best

score is selected. This final tree is passed to the ontological rules, which yield an RDF graph. More on the parser is given in (Anisimovich et al., 2012; Goncharova et al., 2015).

Statistics is gathered on parallel texts, and lexical ambiguity in one language is resolved with the help of other languages.

3.2 Rules

The information extraction system can be considered a rule-based one. The input accepted by the information extraction mechanism is a sequence of syntactic-semantic trees described above (one tree per sentence), the output of the mechanism is an RDF graph. A detailed description of our information extraction module can be found in (Starostin et al., 2014). A rule is itself a condition on parse tree or an object condition (i.e. that an object of a certain type must be "linked" to a certain node in a parse tree). Consider an example:

> Die AfD hat gesagt, dass sie über eine vollständige Alternative verhandeln will.

> *AfD said that it will carry on negotiations regarding a complete alternative.*

Figure 1 shows a fragment of a parse tree generated for the sentence.

```
$Verb, Predicate: ":TO_SAY_SPEAK_TELL_TALK"
   $Subject, Agent: "ACRONYM"
      $Article: ":ARTICLES"
```

Figure 1: Parse tree fragment

Figure 2 shows an example of a rule that would extract an organization on the fragment "AfD".

```
"COMMUNICATION_AND_SPEECH_ACTIVITY"
    [
       Agent: name "ACRONYM"
    ]
=>
Organization Org (name);
```

Figure 2: Rule

The main advantage of this approach is that the rules become language independent. Thus, we could reuse the set of rules that we use for both

English and Russian for German. However, German capitalization was a challenge: in English and Russian capitalization is a good marker to discriminate between abstract and named entities:

1. relationship between Church and State in the Middle Ages

2. He went to church on Sunday

In German this marker does not work because all nouns are capitalized. So far we have decided to create an extra rule, which checks if the noun has dependent adjectives that are capitalized. If such adjectives can be found, the entity is labelled as named, otherwise, the entity is labeled as abstract. The approach, however, works only for part of the cases and tends to miss out correct named entities (consider the example above).

As we evaluated our system on GermEval corpus, we wrote some additional rules to extract entities which are specific to this corpus, i.e. OTHER, ENTITYderiv and ENTITYpart (Benikova et al., 2014). The rules for extraction entities of the type OTHER included conditions on currency names, bracketed names, urls and so on. To extract ENTITYpart type we added a rule that marked the constituent that had the "Composite" grammeme.

Extracting of ENTITYderiv type of entities is challenging for us, because our system rests upon the hierarchy of semantic meanings and does not preserve information that some word was derived from another. For instance, the words "Deutscher" and "Deutsch" are not connected in the hierarchy. We created a rule that added a "deriv" tag to the names of nationalities and to named entities, which were extracted on adjectives.

We did not extract any gazetteers from the corpus, although we plan to do it in the future.

4 Issues

Extending our system to German, we have faced a number of challenges. In this section we will discuss them and offer solutions where possible.

4.1 Organization names

Organization-denoting expressions can have different syntactic structures.

Syntactic structures can be classified as follows. In the easiest case there is: generic word (*Inc., Ltd., GmbH* etc.) and the name of organization in quotes or italics/bold. See below a text example and our structure of its fragment:

"Deutsche Post" AG ist eine große Firma.

ist → AG → #BracketedProperName → AG.

2. In the second case, there is only the name of organization in quotes or italics/bold without a generic word. Ex.:

"Deutsche Post" ist eine große Firma.

Deutsche Post ist eine große Firma.

ist → AG → #BracketedProperName → Post.

3. The third case is similar to the first one, but the name of organization does not have quotes or formatting. Ex.:

Deutsche Post AG ist eine große Firma.

Alpha Versicherung GmbH ist auch eine Firma.

Here we can easily identify only one of the two borders of the named entity, the one where the generic name is. The other border is harder to guess: in the examples above it can be either "Post AG" or "Deutsche Post AG" and "Versicherung GmbH" or "Alpha Versicherung GmbH".

In such cases elements of organization name in English and Russian are normally capitalized, and a dummy node #CapitalizedProperName, an analogue of #BracketedProperName, can be identified on the basis of this capitalization. Ex.:

I shop at Healthy Soups.

shop → #CapitalizedProperName → Soups → Healthy

In German this does not work. Thus we reworked our system and introduced direct links between the generic word and (the main word of) organization title as such.

Organization name itself can belong to one of the several categories (ranked from easier to more difficult):

1. Proper name present in the dictionary. Ex.: "Raiffeisen Bank".

2. Unknown word, i.e. not present in the dictionary. Ex.: "Gruffalo Bank".

3. Common name present in the dictionary in one or more meanings. Ex.: "Deutsche Versicherung Bank".

In the first case, the name helps building the correct structure because the model takes into account correlation statistics between the semantic class of the child node and semantically labelled link, and the statistics for a proper organization name and the link between it and the generic company name is normally good. In the third case the title is misleading because "Versicherung" (insurance) is a common verb noun, which is not a typical child of a *Name* link. Yet, as we cannot use a dummy node in this case in German, we have created a new semantically labelled link between generic company names and this type of organization titles that would allow for such connection. (This work is now in progress.) In this way German has forced us to face this problem. With only English and Russian, such cases were infrequent and could be ignored.

4. In the most difficult case there is neither generic word nor quotes/formatting. Ex.:

Deutsche Post ist eine große Firma.

In this case identification of both borders and thus the very presence of organization name is troublesome. Yet, from our experience, this type is not less frequent.

4.2 Composites

When analyzing a word form, the parser can have several hypotheses about its lemma. If the word can in theory be split into several known word forms, the parser may try to analyze it as a composite word. While it is generally reasonable for a language so rich in composites as German, it may cause problems when analyzing unknown proper names (not present in the dictionary). The inner structure of proper names, particularly person or location names, can be rather complicated: "Tempelhof", "Schimmelmann" etc., yet such words should be treated as single lemmas. But there are also common nouns that are actual composites and that should be split into parts during the analysis: "Tempelarchitektur" (temple architecture), "Schimmelkultur" (fungus culture). In both cases the parser will have two hypotheses for these words: 1) an unknown word (*Tempelhof, Tempelarchitektur*); 2) a composite consisting of several known parts: *Tempel + Architektur*; *Tempel + Hof*. Thus, choosing the correct hypothesis may be challenging.

4.3 Non-German fragments

We have also observed that sequences of foreign words incorporated in German text can create problems for named entity recognition. If none of the foreign words in a sequence looks like a German word, they will all be interpreted as unknown words, which is the best variant in this situation. But if any of the foreign words in the sequence is homonymous to any known word form in German, the parser is more likely to interpret this word as a known German lexeme rather than an unknown one and build a syntactic structure based on this interpretation. This results in incorrect parsing, impeding NE identification. Example: "Zimbabwe Conservation Task Force". The word "Force" is present in the German dictionary as a town name, and the parser can recognize this word form as a location name instead of an element of a sequence of unknown words that together form the name of an organization. A possible solution here is to detect borders of a foreign language fragment and treat all words within it as one unknown item. Yet, this will not a complete solution because there are cases when a German word is incorporated into a foreign language string, which makes border detection more difficult:

Nutzung von Business-zu-Customer-Beziehungen

Here "zu" is a German word, but "customer" and probably "business" are English fragments.

4.4 Abbreviations

Besides high lexical ambiguity resulting from capitalization of all nouns (ex., a noun "Kraft" can be either a common noun or a family name), German also features heavy use of ambiguous abbreviations. For example, "AG" can stand both for "Aktionsgesellschaft" (joint stock company) or "Auftraggeber" (customer). If an abbreviation has a limited number of interpretations or several most frequent interpretations, it can be placed in the dictionary in several meanings. And then disambiguation can be helped by the context: if "AG" is an object of "gründen", the statistical score for the combination of "gründen" + company will be better than for "gründen" + person. But if an abbreviation has an unlimited number of meanings that are relatively equally frequent, it is impossible to include all of them into the dictionary, and it makes little sense to include only some of meanings. In such cases the abbreviation is not included it into the dictionary, and is interpreted as an unknown acronym at the parsing stage.

4.5 Quotation marks

If a fragment of text has quotation marks around it, there is a high probability that it denotes a named entity such as an organization name. However, quotation marks can also be used in some other contexts such as quoting: "'Excuse me', the boy said". For the languages we have previously dealt with we can look up for speech verbs in order to disambiguate between the two usages of quotation marks. However, for German the presence of a speech verb is not always obligatory since there exists a special verb form (Konjunktiv I) designating reported speech. Thus for a fragment in a long sequence of Konjunktiv I sentences quotation marks can signify either reported speech or a named entity, even if there is not any speech verb nearby.

5 Evaluation

Precision (%)	Recall (%)	FB1 (%)
45.22	44.87	45.04

Table 1: Overall results. Strict metric

We have tested our system on GermEval 2014 corpus using the evaluation script provided by the organizers. Overall results of strict evaluation are presented in Table 1, results of strict evaluation by categories are given in Tables 2, 3, 4, 5. Predictably, extraction of organizations has turned out to be the most challenging task for us, due to the parsing problems mentioned above. We hope that the implementation of changes to the parser suggested in Section 4 will improve the quality of parse trees and entity extraction. Enrichment of Organization gazetteer is also likely to help.

	Precision	Recall	FB1
PER (outer)	63.02	65.68	64.33
PER (inner)	30.43	20.59	24.56
PERpart (outer)	0	0	0
PERpart(inner)	0	0	0
PERderiv(outer)	0	0	0
PERderiv (inner)	0	0	0

Table 2: Results for PER (in %)

	Precision	Recall	FB1
LOC (outer)	78.5	49.28	60.55
LOC (inner)	15.38	9.43	11.7
LOCpart (outer)	50.94	51.92	51.43
LOCpart(inner)	8.33	100	15.38
LOCderiv(outer)	88.46	39.15	54.28
LOCderiv (inner)	28.57	17.02	21.33

Table 3: Results for LOC (in %)

	Precision	Recall	FB1
ORG (outer)	18.7	32.46	23.73
ORG (inner)	0	0	0
ORGpart (outer)	77.14	29.67	42.86
ORGpart(inner)	0	0	0
ORGderiv(outer)	0	0	0
ORGderiv (inner)	0	0	0

Table 4: Results for ORG (in %)

The results of "Person" type extraction are quite unexpected, first of all, because recall-better-than-precision pattern is not typical for us. These results require further analysis, which is beyond the scope of this paper.

The precision of "Location" type extraction is relatively high and we believe that further Location gazetteer enrichment will improve the recall considerably.

6 Conclusions

In this paper we presented our rule-based approach to named entity recognition for the German language. The approach has previously been applied to Russian and English languages and has shown good results. However, we have found out that several changes should be made to the parser to obtain better results on German. We have evaluated our system on GermEval 2014 corpus and presented the results as well as the analysis of problems we as a parser- and rule-based system have faced. In the nearest future we plan to implement several changes to the parser as well as enrich organizations and locations gazetteers in order to obtain better results for German.

References

K.V. Anisimovich, K.Ju. Druzhkin, F.R. Minlos, M.A. Petrova, V.P. Selegey, and K.A. Zuev. 2012. Syntactic and semantic parser based on ABBYY Compreno linguistic technologies. In *Computational*

	Precision	**Recall**	**FB1**
OTH (outer)	39.34	39.78	39.56
OTH (inner)	0	0	0
OTHpart (outer)	12.9	22.22	16.33
OTHpart(inner)	0	0	0
OTHderiv(outer)	33.33	50	40
OTHderiv (inner)	0	0	0

Table 5: Results for OTH (in %)

Linguistics and Intellectual Technologies. Papers from the Annual International Conference «Dialogue» (2012), number 11, pages 91–103.

Darina Benikova, Chris Biemann, Max Kisselew, and Sebastian Padó. 2014. GermEval 2014 Named Entity Recognition Shared Task: Companion Paper. In *Proceedings of the KONVENS GermEval workshop*, pages 104–112, Hildesheim, Germany.

Yulia Bobkova, Andreas Scholz, Tetiana Teplynska, and Desislava Zhekova. 2014. HATNER: Nested Named Entitiy Recognition for German. *Proceedings of the KONVENS GermEval Shared Task on Named Entity Recognition, Hildesheim, Germany*.

C. Fellbaum. 1998. *WordNet: An Electronic Lexical Database*. Language, speech, and communication. MIT Press.

M.B. Goncharova, E.A. Kozlova, A.V. Pasyukov, R.V. Garashchuk, and V.P. Selegey. 2015. Model-based WSA as means of new language integration into a multilingual lexical-semantic database with interlingua. In *Computational Linguistics and Intellectual Technologies. Papers from the Annual International Conference «Dialogue» (2015)*, volume 1, pages 169–182.

Ralph Grishman. 2003. Information Extraction. *The Handbook of Computational Linguistics and Natural Language Processing*, pages 515–530.

Martin Hermann, Michael Hochleitner, Sarah Kellner, Simon Preissner, and Desislava Zhekova. 2014. Nessy: A Hybrid Approach to Named Entity Recognition for German. *Proceedings of the KONVENS GermEval Shared Task on Named Entity Recognition, Hildesheim, Germany*.

Joakim Nivre, 2015. *Computational Linguistics and Intelligent Text Processing: 16th International Conference, CICLing 2015, Cairo, Egypt, April 14-20, 2015, Proceedings, Part I*, chapter Towards a Universal Grammar for Natural Language Processing, pages 3–16. Springer International Publishing, Cham.

A.S. Starostin, I.M. Smurov, and M.E. Stepanova. 2014. A Production System for Information Extraction Based on Complete Syntactic-semantic Analysis. In *Computational Linguistics and Intellectual Technologies. Papers from the Annual International Conference «Dialogue» (2014)*, pages 659–667.

A.S. Starostin, V.V. Bocharov, S.V. Alexeeva, A.A. Bodrova, A.S. Chuchunkov, S.S. Dzhumaev, I.V. Efimenko, D.V. Granovsky, V.F. Khoroshevsky, I.V. Krylova, M.A. Nikolaeva, I.M. Smurov, and S.Y. Toldova. 2016. FactRuEval 2016: Evaluation of Named Entity Recognition and Fact Extraction Systems for Russian. In *Computational Linguistics and Intellectual Technologies. Proceedings of the Annual International Conference «Dialogue» (2016)*, number 15, pages 702–720.

M.E. Stepanova, E.A Budnikov, A.N. Chelombeeva, P.V. Matavina, and D.A. Skorinkin. 2016. Information Extraction Based on Deep Syntactic-Semantic Analysis. In *Computational Linguistics and Intellectual Technologies. Proceedings of the Annual International Conference «Dialogue» (2016)*, number 15, pages 721–732.

Erik F Tjong Kim Sang and Fien De Meulder. 2003. Introduction to the CoNLL-2003 shared task: Language-independent named entity recognition. In *Proceedings of the seventh conference on Natural language learning at HLT-NAACL 2003-Volume 4*, pages 142–147. Association for Computational Linguistics.

Patrick Watrin, Louis de Viron, Denis Lebailly, Matthieu Constant, and Stephanie Weiser. 2014. Named Entity Recognition for German Using Conditional Random Fields and Linguistic Resources. *Proceedings of the KONVENS GermEval Shared Task on Named Entity Recognition, Hildesheim, Germany*.

Daniel Weber and Josef Pötzl. 2014. NERU: Named Entity Recognition for German. *Proceedings of the KONVENS GermEval Shared Task on Named Entity Recognition, Hildesheim, Germany*.

Spanish NER with Word Representations and Conditional Random Fields

Jenny Copara[1], Jose Ochoa[1], Camilo Thorne[2], Goran Glavaš[2]
[1]Universidad Católica San Pablo, Arequipa, Peru
{jenny.copara,jeochoa}@ucsp.edu.pe
[2]Data & Web Science Group, Universität Mannheim, Germany
{camilo,goran}@informatik.uni-mannheim.de

Abstract

Word Representations such as word embeddings have been shown to significantly improve (semi-)supervised NER for the English language. In this work we investigate whether word representations can also boost (semi-)supervised NER in Spanish. To do so, we use word representations as additional features in a linear chain Conditional Random Field (CRF) classifier. Experimental results (82.44 F-score on the CoNLL-2002 corpus) show that our approach is comparable to some state-of-the-art Deep Learning approaches for Spanish, in particular when using cross-lingual Word Representations.

Keywords. NER for Spanish, Word Representations, Conditional Random Fields.

1 Introduction

Supervised NER models require large amounts of (manually) labeled data to achieve good performance, data that often is hard to acquire or generate. However, it is possible to take advantage of unlabeled data to learn word representations to enrich and boost supervised NER models learned over small gold standards.

In supervised NER the common practice has been to use domain-specific lexicon (list of words related with named entity types) (Carreras et al., 2002; Ratinov and Roth, 2009; Passos et al., 2014). More recently, it has been shown that supervised NER can be boosted via specific word features induced from very large unsupervised word representations (Turian et al., 2010), and in particular, from **(i)** very large word clusters (Brown et al., 1992; Liang, 2005), and **(ii)** very large word embeddings (Collobert and Weston, 2008; Mikolov et al., 2013a; Mikolov et al.,

2013b; dos Santos and Guimarães, 2015). For English NER, (Passos et al., 2014; Guo et al., 2014) show that (large) word embeddings yield better results than clustering. However, when combined and fed as features to linear chain conditional random field (CRF) sequence classifiers, they yield models comparable to state-of-the-art deep learning approaches, but with the added value of a very large coverage (Guo et al., 2014).

In this paper we investigate whether these techniques can be successfully applied to NER in Spanish. In order to do so, we follow Guo et al. (2014)'s approach combining probabilistic graphical models learned from the CoNLL 2002 corpus, with word representations learned from large unlabeled Spanish corpora, while exploring the optimal setting and feature combinations that match state-of-the-art algorithms for NER in Spanish.

The paper is organized as follows. In Section 2, we provide a review of Spanish NER, and NER using word representations as features. Section 3 describes the structure of the word representations used. Section 4 shows our experimental setting and results. Section 5 presents our final remarks.

2 Related work

2.1 Spanish NER

The first results (CoNLL 2002 shared-task[1]) for (supervised) Spanish NER were obtained by Carreras et al. (2002) where a set of selected word features and lexicons (gazetteers) on an Adaboost learning model were used, obtaining an F-score of 81.39%. These results remained unbeaten until recently, and the spread of *Deep Learning*. The state-of-the-art algorithms for this task (currently achieving an F-score of 85.77%) are mostly based on Deep Learning. Convolutional Neural Networks with word and character embeddings (dos

---

[1]http://www.cnts.ua.ac.be/conll2002/ner/

Proceedings of the Sixth Named Entity Workshop, joint with 54th ACL, pages 34–40,
Berlin, Germany, August 12, 2016. ©2016 Association for Computational Linguistics

Santos and Guimarães, 2015), Recurrent Neural Networks (RNNs) with word and character embeddings (Lample et al., 2016; Yang et al., 2016), and a character-based RNN with characters encoded as bytes (Gillick et al., 2015).

2.2 Word Representations

Word Representations have been shown to substantially improve several NLP tasks, among which NER for English and German (Faruqui and Padó, 2010).

There are two main approaches. One approach is to compute clusters (Brown et al., 1992; Liang, 2005) (Brown Clustering) from unlabeled data and using them as features in NLP models (including NER). Another approach transforms each word into a continuous real-valued vector (Collobert and Weston, 2008) of n dimensions also known as a "word embedding" (Mikolov et al., 2013a). With (Brown) clustering, words that appear in the same or a similar sentence context are assigned to the same cluster. Whereas in word embeddings similar words occur close to each other in $\mathbb{R}^n$ (the induced n dimensional vector space).

Word Representations work better the more data they are fed. One way to achieve this is to input them cross-lingual datasets, provided they overlap in vocabulary and domain. Cross-lingual Word Representations have been shown to improve several NLP tasks, such as model learning(Bhattarai, 2013; Yu et al., 2013a). This is because, among other things, they allow to extend the coverage of possibly limited (in the sense of small or sparsely annotated) resources through Word Representations in other languages. For instance, using English to enrich Chinese (Yu et al., 2013a), or learning a model in English to solve a Text Classification task in German (also German-English, English-French and French-English) (Bhattarai, 2013).

3 Word Representations for Spanish NER

Brown clustering Brown clustering is a hierarchical clustering of words that takes a sequence $w_1, \ldots, w_n$ of words as input and returns a binary tree as output. The binary tree's leaves are the input words. This clustering method is based on bigram language models (Brown et al., 1992; Liang, 2005).

Clustering embeddings A clustering method for embeddings based on *k-means* has been proposed in Yu et al. (2013b). Experiments have shown different numbers for k's which contains different granularity information. The toolkit Sofia-ml (Sculley, 2010) [2] was used to do so.

Binarized embeddings The idea behind this method is to "reduce" continous word vectors $\vec{w}$ in standard word embeddings, into discrete $bin(\vec{w})$ vectors, that however preserve the ordering or ranking of the embeddings. To do this, we need to compute two thresholds per dimension (upper and lower) across the whole vocabulary. For each dimension (component) i of is computed the *mean* of positives values (C_{i+}, the upper threshold) and negative values (C_{i-}, the lower one). Thereafter, the following function is used over each component C_{ij} of vector $\vec{w}_j$:

$$\phi(C_{ij}) = \begin{cases} U_+, & if C_{ij} \geq mean(C_{i+}), \\ B_-, & if C_{ij} \leq mean(C_{i-}), \\ 0, & otherwise. \end{cases}$$

Distributional Prototypes This approach is based on the idea that each entity class has a set of words more likely to belong to this class than the other words (i.e., Maria, Jose are more likely to be classified as a *PERSON* entity). Thus, it is useful to identify a group of words that represent each class (*prototypes*) and select *some of them* in order to use them as word features. In order to compute prototypes Guo et al. (2014) two steps are necessary:

1. Generate a prototype for each class of an annotated training corpus. This step relies on Normalized Pointwise Mutual Information (NPMI) (Bouma, 2009). Word-entity type relations can be modeled as a form of collocation. NPMI is a smoothed version of the Mutual Information measure typically used to detect word associations (Yang and Pedersen, 1997) and collocations. Given an annotated training corpus, the NPMI is computed between labels l and words w using the following two formulas:

$$\lambda_n(l, w) = \frac{\lambda(l, w)}{-\ln p(l, w)}, \quad \lambda(l, w) = \ln \frac{p(l, w)}{p(l)p(w)}.$$

---

[2] https://code.google.com/archive/p/sofia-ml/

2. Map the prototypes to words in a (large) word embedding. In this step, given a group of prototypes for each class, we find out which prototypes in our set are the most *similar* to each word in the embeddings. *Cosine similarity* is used to do so and those prototypes above a threshold of usually 0.5 are chosen as the prototype features of the word.

4   Experiments and Discussion

Unlike previous approaches, our work focuses on using word representations as features for supervised NER for Spanish. We do it within a probabilistic grahical model framework: Conditional Random Fields (CRFs). CRFs allows us to intensively explore available resources (unlabeled data) within a simple graphical model setting (in contrast to complex Deep Learning approaches). We trained our (enriched) model over the (Spanish) CoNLL 2002 corpus, and built our Word Representations over, on the one hand, the Spanish Billion Corpus, and on the other hand, English Wikipedia. For Spanish this is a novel approach. The experimental results show it achieves competitive performance w.r.t. the current (Deep learning-driven) state-of-the-art for Spanish NER, in particular when using *cross-* or *multi-lingual* Word Representations.

4.1   NER Model

We used for our NER experiments a linear chain CRF sequence classifier, whose main properties we briefly recall (for a detailed description of this known model please refer to Sutton and McCallum (2012)). Linear chain CRFs are discrimative probabilistic graphical models that work by estimating the conditional probability of label sequence t given word sequence (sentence) w:

$$p(t|w) = \frac{1}{Z} \exp \left(\sum_{i=1}^{|t|} \sum_{j=1}^{\#(F)} \theta_j f_j(t_{i_1}, t_i, w_i) \right)$$

where Z is a normalization factor that sums the body (argument) of the exponential over all sequences of labels t, the f_js are feature functions and w_i is the word window observed at position i of the input. The parameters θ_j of the model are estimated via so-called gradient minimization methods.

Our classifier relies on a set of standard baseline features, that we extend with additional features

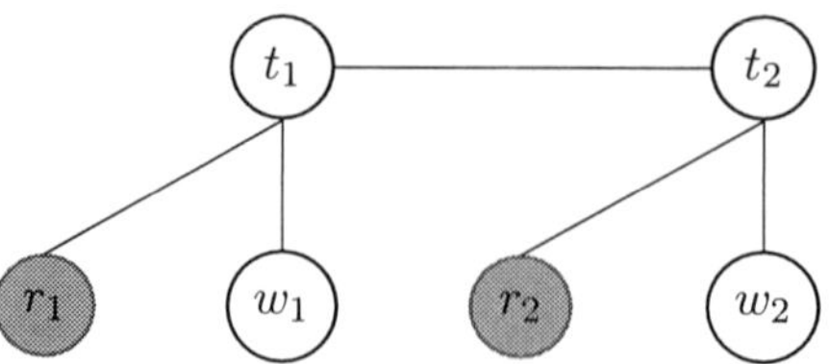

Figure 1: Linear chain-CRF with word representations as features. The upper nodes are the label sequences, the bottom white nodes are the word features in the model and the filled nodes are the word representations features included in our model.

based on word representations in order to take advantage of unlabeled data, as depicted in Figure 1. The classifier was implemented using *CRFSuite* (Okazaki, 2007), due to its simplicity and the ease with which one can add extra features. Additionally, we experimented with the Stanford CRF classifier for NER (Finkel et al., 2005), for comparison purposes.

4.2   Baseline Features

The baseline features were defined over a window of ± *2 tokens*. The set of features for each word was:

- The word itself.
- Lower-case word.
- Part-of-speech tag.
- Capitalization pattern and type of character in the word.
- Characters type information: capitalized, digits, symbols, initial upper case letter, all characters are letters or digits.
- Prefixes and suffixes: four first or latter letters respectively.
- Digit length: whether the current token has 2 or 4 length.
- Digit combination: which digit combination the current token has (alphanumeric, slash, comma, period).
- Whether the current token has just uppercase letter and period mark or contains an uppercase, lowercase, digit, alphanumeric, symbol character.
- Flags for initial letter capitalized, all letter capitalized, all lower case, all digits, all non-alphanumeric characters,

4.3   CoNLL 2002 Spanish Corpus

The CoNLL 2002 shared task (Tjong Kim Sang, 2002) gave rise to a training and evaluation

LOC	MISC	ORG	PER
6 983	2 958	10 490	6 278

Table 1: Entities in CoNLL-2002 (Spanish).

standard for supervised NER algorithms used ever since: the CoNLL-2002 Spanish corpus. The CoNLL is tagged with four entities: *PERSON, ORGANIZATION, LOCATION, MISCELLANEOUS* and nine classes: B-PER, I-PER, B-ORG, I-ORG, B-LOC, I-LOC, B-MISC, I-MISC and O. In this corpus there are 74 683 tokens and 11 755 sentences. Additional information about the entities in the corpus is shown in Table 1.

4.4 Word Representations

Spanish Dataset In order to compute our word representations (viz., the Brown clusters and word embeddings) a large amount of unlabeled data is required. To this end we relied on the Spanish Billion Words (SBW) corpus and embeddings (Cardellino, 2016). This dataset was gathered from several public domain resources [3] in Spanish: e.g., a Spanish portion of SenSem, the Ancora Corpus, the Europarl and OPUS Project Corpora, the Tibidabo Treebank and IULA Spanish LSP Treebank and dumps from Spanish Wikipedia, Wikisource and Wikibooks until September 2015 (Cardellino, 2016). The corpora cover 3 817 833 *unique* tokens, and the embeddings 1 000 653 *unique* tokens with 300 dimensions per vector.

Cross-lingual Dataset Entity names tend to be very similar (often, identical) across languages and domains. This should imply that Word Representation approaches should gain in performance when cross- or multi-lingual datasets are used. To test this hypothesis, we used an English Wikipedia dump from 2012 preprocessed by Guo et al. (2014), who removed paragraphs that contained non-roman characters and lowercased words. Additionally they removed frequent words.

Brown clustering The number k of word clusters for Brown clustering was fixed to 1000 following Turian et al. (2010). Sample Brown clusters are shown in Table 2. The cluster is used as feature of each word in the annotated CoNLL 2002. As the reader can see Brown clustering tends to

Brown Clusters	Word
011100010	Française
011100010	Hamburg
011100010	Peru
0111100011010	latino
0111100011010	sueco
0111100011010	conservador
0111111001111	malogran
0111111001111	paralizaban
011101001010	Facebook
011101001010	Twitter
011101001010	Internet

Table 2: Brown cluster computed from SBW.

Dimension	Value	Binarized
1	-0.008255	0
2	-0.013051	0
3	0.145529	U+
4	0.010853	0
$\vdots$	$\vdots$	$\vdots$
295	0.050766	U+
296	-0.066613	B-
297	0.073499	U+
298	-0.034749	0
299	-0.023611	0
300	-0.025693	0

Table 3: Binarized embeddings from SBW for word "equipo".

assign the entities to the same type to the same cluster.

Binarized Embeddings Table 3 shows a short view of word "equipo". In the first column we can see each dimension of "equipo" and in the second its continuous value. The third column shows the binarized value. We used the binarized value as features for each observed word (all dimensions with a *binarized value* different to *zero* will be considered).

Clustering Embeddings For cluster embeddings, 500, 1000, 1500, 2000 and 3000 clusters were computed, to model different levels of granularity (Guo et al., 2014). As features for each word w, we return the cluster assignments at each granularity level. Table 4 shows the clusters of embeddings computed for word "Maria". The first column denotes the level of granularity. The second column denotes the cluster assigned to "Maria" at

---

[3] http://crscardellino.me/SBWCE/

Granularity	k
500	31
1000	978
1500	1317
2000	812
3000	812

Table 4: Clustering embeddings from SBW for word "Maria".

Class	Prototypes
B-ORG	EFE, Gobierno, PP, Ayuntamiento
I-ORG	Nacional, Europea, Unidos, Civil
I-MISC	Campeones, Ambiente, Ciudadana, Profesional
B-MISC	Liga, Copa, Juegos, Internet
B-LOC	Madrid, Barcelona, Badajoz, Santander
I-LOC	Janeiro, York, Denis, Aires
B-PER	Francisco, Juan, Fernando, Manuel
I-PER	Alvarez, Lozano, Bosque, Ibarra
O	que, el, en, y

Table 5: CoNLL-2002 Spanish Prototypes.

Model	F1
Baseline	80.02%
+Binarization	79.48%
+Brown	80.99%
+Prototype	79.82%
+Clustering	80.24%
+Clustering+Prototype	80.55%
+Brown+Clustering	82.30%
+Brown+Clustering+Prototype	81.19%
+Brown+Clustering+Prototype*	**82.44%**
Carreras et al. (2002)[†]	79.28%
Carreras et al. (2002)	81.39%
Finkel et al. (2005)	81.44%
dos Santos and Guimarães (2015)	82.21%
Gillick et al. (2015)	82.95%
Lample et al. (2016)	85.75%
Yang et al. (2016)	85.77%

[*]Brown clusters from English resource
[†]did not take into in account gazetteers

Table 6: CoNLL2002 Spanish Results. Top: results obtained by us. Middle: results obtained with other CRF-based approaches. Down: current Deep Learning-based state-of-the-art for Spanish NER.

each granularity level.

Distributional Prototypes Regarding prototypes, we extracted, for each CoNLL BIO label 40 prototypes (the top most 40 w.r.t. NPMI).

Table 5 shows the top four prototypes per entity class computed from CoNLL-2002 Spanish corpus (training subset). These prototypes are instances of each entity class even non-entity tag (O) and therefore they are compound by entities or entity parts (i.e. *Buenos Aires* is a *LOCATION* so we see the word *Aires* as prototype of I-LOC).

4.5 Results

In order to evaluate our models we used the standard `conlleval`[4] script. Table 6 shows the results achieved on CoNLL-2002 (Spanish), and compares them to Stanford and the state-of-the-art for Spanish NER. The Baseline achieved 80.02% of F-score.

It is worth nothing that *Brown clustering* improves the baseline. The same holds for *Clustered embeddings*. By contrast, *Binarization embeddings* does worse than the *Baseline*. This seems

to be due to the fact that binarized embeddings by grouping vector components into a finite set of discrete values throw away information relevant for Spanish NER. The same goes for *Prototypes*, which when taken alone yield results also below the *Baseline*.

Combining the features, on the other hand, yields in all cases results above the baseline, as well as above Brown clustering and clustered embeddings alone.

However, our best results were obtained by using a *cross-lingual combination* combining Brown clusters computed from the English Wikipedia dump (2012) with clustered embeddings and prototypes computed from SBW. The reason Brown clusters are good in this task is due to the high level of overlap among entities in Spanish and English. Put otherwise, many entities that share the same name and a similar context occur in texts from both languages, giving rise to features with higher predictive value.

4.6 Discussion

The first results for supervised Spanish NER using the CoNLL 2002 corpus considered a set of features with gazetteers and external knowl-

---

[4]http://www.cnts.ua.ac.be/conll2000/chunking/conlleval.txt

edge Carreras et al. (2002) which turned out 81.39% F1-score (see Table 6). However, without gazetteers and external knowledge results go down to 79.28% (see Table 6).

It is worth noting that the knowledge injected to the previous learning model was *supervised*. We on the other hand have considered *unsupervised* external knowledge, while significantly improving on those results. This is further substantiated by our exploring unsupervised features with the Stanford NER CRF model (Finkel et al., 2005). In this setting F-score of 81.44% was obtained, again above Carreras et al. (2002).

More importantly, our work shows that an English resource (Brown clusters computed from English Wikipedia) can be used to improve Spanish NER with Word Representations as *(i)* entities in Spanish and English are often identical, and *(ii)* the resulting English Brown clusters for English entities correlate better with their entity types, giving rise to a better model.

Another point to note is that while binarization improves on English NER baselines Guo et al. (2014), the same does not work for Spanish. It seems that this approach adds instead noise to Spanish NER

We also note that *word capitalization* has a distinct impact on our approach. With the following setting: English Brown clusters, Spanish cluster embeddings and *lowercased* Spanish prototypes we got 0.78% less F-score than with uppercased prototypes. This is because the lowercased prototypes will ignore the real context in which the entity appears (since a prototype is an instance of an entity class) and will be therefore mapped to the wrong word vector in the embedding (when computing cosine similarity).

Finally, when comparing our approach to the current state-of-the-art using Deep Learning methods (dos Santos and Guimarães, 2015; Gillick et al., 2015; Lample et al., 2016; Yang et al., 2016) (that extract features at the character, word and bytecode level to learn deep models), our work outperforms dos Santos and Guimarães (2015) F-score and matches also Gillick et al. (2015).

5 Conclusions

This paper has explored unsupervised and minimally supervised features, based on cross-lingual Word Representations, within a CRF classification model for Spanish NER, trained over the Span-ish CoNLL 2002 corpus, the Spanish Billion Word Corpus and English Wikipedia (2012 dump). This is a novel approach for Spanish. Our experiments show competitive results when compared to the current state-of-the-art in Spanish NER, based on Deep Learning, while increasing the coverage of the model. In particular, we outmatcht dos Santos and Guimarães (2015).

Cross-lingual Word Representations have a positive impact on NER performance for Spanish. In the future, we would like to focus further on this aspect and consider more (large scale) cross-lingual datasets.

Acknowledgments

We thank Data and Web Science Group in particular Heiner Stuckenschmidt and Simone Ponzetto for useful help. This work was supported by the Master Program in Computer Science of the Universidad Católica San Pablo and the Peruvian National Fund of Scientific and Technological Development through grant number 011-2013-FONDECYT.

References

Binod Bhattarai. 2013. Inducing cross-lingual word representations. Master's thesis, Multimodal Computing and Interaction, Machine Learning for Natural Language Processing. Universität des Saarlandes.

G. Bouma. 2009. Normalized (pointwise) mutual information in collocation extraction. In C. Chiarcos, E. de Castilho, and M. Stede, editors, *Von der Form zur Bedeutung: Texte automatisch verarbeiten / From Form to Meaning: Processing Texts Automatically, Proceedings of the Biennial GSCL Conference 2009*, pages 31–40, Tübingen. Gunter Narr Verlag.

Peter F. Brown, Peter V. deSouza, Robert L. Mercer, Vincent J. Della Pietra, and Jenifer C. Lai. 1992. Class-based n-gram models of natural language. *Comput. Linguist.*, 18(4):467–479, December.

Cristian Cardellino. 2016. Spanish Billion Words Corpus and Embeddings, March.

Xavier Carreras, Lluís Màrques, and Lluís Padró. 2002. Named entity extraction using adaboost. In *Proceedings of CoNLL-2002*, pages 167–170. Taipei, Taiwan.

Ronan Collobert and Jason Weston. 2008. A unified architecture for natural language processing: Deep neural networks with multitask learning. In *Proceedings of the 25th International Conference on Machine Learning*, ICML '08, pages 160–167, New York, NY, USA. ACM.

Cicero dos Santos and Victor Guimarães. 2015. Boosting named entity recognition with neural character embeddings. In *Proceedings of the Fifth Named Entity Workshop*, pages 25–33, Beijing, China, July. Association for Computational Linguistics.

Manaal Faruqui and Sebastian Padó. 2010. Training and evaluating a german named entity recognizer with semantic generalization. In *Proceedings of KONVENS 2010*, Saarbrücken, Germany.

Jenny Rose Finkel, Trond Grenager, and Christopher Manning. 2005. Incorporating non-local information into information extraction systems by gibbs sampling. In *Proceedings of the 43rd Annual Meeting on Association for Computational Linguistics*, ACL '05, pages 363–370, Stroudsburg, PA, USA. Association for Computational Linguistics.

D. Gillick, C. Brunk, O. Vinyals, and A. Subramanya. 2015. Multilingual Language Processing From Bytes. *ArXiv e-prints*, November.

Jiang Guo, Wanxiang Che, Haifeng Wang, and Ting Liu. 2014. Revisiting embedding features for simple semi-supervised learning. In *Proceedings of the 2014 Conference on Empirical Methods in Natural Language Processing (EMNLP)*, pages 110–120, Doha, Qatar, October. Association for Computational Linguistics.

Guillaume Lample, Miguel Ballesteros, Kazuya Kawakami, Sandeep Subramanian, and Chris Dyer. 2016. Neural architectures for named entity recognition. In *In proceedings of NAACL-HLT (NAACL 2016).*, San Diego, US.

Percy Liang. 2005. Semi-supervised learning for natural language. Master's thesis, Department of Electrical Engineering and Computer Science. Massachusetts Institute of Technology.

Tomas Mikolov, Kai Chen, Greg Corrado, and Jeffrey Dean. 2013a. Efficient estimation of word representations in vector space. *CoRR*, abs/1301.3781.

Tomas Mikolov, Ilya Sutskever, Kai Chen, Greg S. Corrado, and Jeff Dean. 2013b. Distributed representations of words and phrases and their compositionality. In C.j.c. Burges, L. Bottou, M. Welling, Z. Ghahramani, and K.q. Weinberger, editors, *Advances in Neural Information Processing Systems 26*, pages 3111–3119.

Naoaki Okazaki. 2007. Crfsuite: a fast implementation of conditional random fields (crfs).

Alexandre Passos, Vineet Kumar, and Andrew McCallum. 2014. Lexicon infused phrase embeddings for named entity resolution. In *Proceedings of the Eighteenth Conference on Computational Natural Language Learning*, pages 78–86, Ann Arbor, Michigan, June. Association for Computational Linguistics.

Lev Ratinov and Dan Roth. 2009. Design challenges and misconceptions in named entity recognition. In *Proceedings of the Thirteenth Conference on Computational Natural Language Learning*, CoNLL '09, pages 147–155, Stroudsburg, PA, USA. Association for Computational Linguistics.

D. Sculley. 2010. Combined regression and ranking. In *Proceedings of the 16th ACM SIGKDD International Conference on Knowledge Discovery and Data Mining*, KDD '10, pages 979–988, New York, NY, USA. ACM.

Charles Sutton and Andrew McCallum. 2012. An introduction to conditional random fields. *Foundations and Trends in Machine Learning*, 4(4):267–373.

Erik F. Tjong Kim Sang. 2002. Introduction to the conll-2002 shared task: Language-independent named entity recognition. In *Proceedings of the 6th Conference on Natural Language Learning - Volume 20*, COLING-02, pages 1–4, Stroudsburg, PA, USA. Association for Computational Linguistics.

Joseph Turian, Lev Ratinov, and Yoshua Bengio. 2010. Word representations: A simple and general method for semi-supervised learning. In *Proceedings of the 48th Annual Meeting of the Association for Computational Linguistics*, ACL '10, pages 384–394, Stroudsburg, PA, USA. Association for Computational Linguistics.

Yiming Yang and Jan O. Pedersen. 1997. A comparative study on feature selection in text categorization. In *Proceedings of the Fourteenth International Conference on Machine Learning*, ICML '97, pages 412–420, San Francisco, CA, USA. Morgan Kaufmann Publishers Inc.

Zhilin Yang, Ruslan Salakhutdinov, and William Cohen. 2016. Multi-task cross-lingual sequence tagging from scratch. *CoRR*, abs/1603.06270.

Mo Yu, Tiejun Zhao, Yalong Bai, Hao Tian, and Dianhai Yu. 2013a. Cross-lingual projections between languages from different families. In *Proceedings of the 51st Annual Meeting of the Association for Computational Linguistics (Volume 2: Short Papers)*, pages 312–317, Sofia, Bulgaria, August. Association for Computational Linguistics.

Mo Yu, Tiejun Zhao, Daxiang Dong, Hao Tian, and Dianhai Yu. 2013b. Compound embedding features for semi-supervised learning. In *Human Language Technologies: Conference of the North American Chapter of the Association of Computational Linguistics, Proceedings, June 9-14, 2013, Westin Peachtree Plaza Hotel, Atlanta, Georgia, USA*, pages 563–568.

Constructing a Japanese Basic Named Entity Corpus of Various Genres

Tomoya Iwakura[1], Ryuichi Tachibana [2], and Kanako Komiya [3]

[1] Fujitsu Laboratories Ltd. [2] Commerce Link Inc. [3] Ibaraki University

Abstract

This paper introduces a Japanese Named Entity (NE) corpus of various genres. We annotated 136 documents in the Balanced Corpus of Contemporary Written Japanese (BCCWJ) with the eight types of NE tags defined by Information Retrieval and Extraction Exercise. The NE corpus consists of six types of genres of documents such as blogs, magazines, white papers, and so on, and the corpus contains 2,464 NE tags in total. The corpus can be reproduced with BCCWJ corpus and the tagging information obtained from https://sites.google.com/ site/projectnextnlpne/en/ .

1 Introduction

Named Entity (NE) recognition is a process by which the names of particular classes and numeric expressions are recognized in text. NEs include person names, locations, organizations, dates, times, and so on. NE recognition is one of the basic technologies used in text processing, including Information Extraction (IE), Question Answering (QA), and Information Retrieval (IR).

For the development of NE recognizers in early stage, newspaper articles have been mainly used. For example, the following data sets consist of newspaper articles: eight types of basic Japanese NE recognition data sets for Information Retrieval and Extraction Exercise (IREX) (IREX Committee, 1999), the CoNLL'03 shared task (Tjong Kim Sang and De Meulder, 2003), an English fine-grained NE type that includes 64 classes (Weischedel and Brunstein, 2005), and Sekine's extended NE hierarchy that includes about 200 classes of NEs (Sekine et al., 2002).

As for Sekine's extended NE hierarchy, NE corpus have been created on various genres documents such as blogs, white papers and so on, in BCCWJ (Maekawa et al., 2010).[1] However, compared with the corpus for Sekine's extended NE hierarchy, which covers several genres, corpus for Japanese basic NEs have been created for fewer genres of documents such as newspaper articles of IREX and leading sentences of Web pages (Hangyo et al., 2012).

This paper introduces a Japanese Named Entity (NE) corpus of various genres called BCCWJ Basic NE corpus. BCCWJ Basic NE corpus was created for the sake of expanding genres of documents for Japanese basic NE researches. The corpus includes 136 documents in the Balanced Corpus of Contemporary Written Japanese (BCCWJ) core data annotated with the eight types of NE tags defined by IREX. The corpus contains 2,464 NE tags in total and the genres of the documents are following: Yahoo! Chiebukuro (OC)[2], White Paper (OW), Yahoo! Blog (OY), Books (PB), Magazines (PM) and Newspapers (PN). This corpus includes genres of documents that have not been targeted in existing NE corpus for IREX definition. (IREX Committee, 1999; Hangyo et al., 2012).

2 IREX NE Definition

IREX committee defined the eight NE types: ARTIFACT, LOCATION, ORGANIZATION, PERSON, DATE, MONEY, PERCENT and TIME. Table 1 shows the eight NE types and their examples. In addition to the eight NE types, OPTIONAL, for ambiguous NEs, were defined.

For example, from the following sentence, "Mr. Miyazaki comes from Miyazaki." in English, an

---

[1] The IREX definition is not a subset of the Sekine's extended NE hierarchy.

[2] Yahoo! Chiebukuro consists documents from a QA site on the Web.

Proceedings of the Sixth Named Entity Workshop, joint with 54th ACL, pages 41–46,
Berlin, Germany, August 12, 2016. ©2016 Association for Computational Linguistics

NE type	Example
ARTIFACT	Nobel Prize
LOCATION	Japan
ORGANIZATION	Foreign Ministry
PERSON	Tom White
DATE	May, 5th
MONEY	100 yen
PERCENT	100%
TIME	10:00 p.m.

Table 1: The eight NE types defined by IREX and the examples.

NE recognizer should extract the first Miyazaki as PERSON and the second one as LOCATION because NE types are decided by context in the IREX definition.

$\langle PER \rangle$ 宮崎 $\langle /PER \rangle$ さん   は
(Miyazaki)   (Mr.)   (postposition)
$\langle LOC \rangle$ 宮崎 $\langle /LOC \rangle$ 出身
(Miyazaki)   (comes from)

PER and LOC in the above example indicate PERSON and LOCATION.

3 BCCWJ Basic NE corpus

We annotated 136 documents included in BCCWJ core data with IREX-defined NE tags by the following procedure.[3] We choose the same documents of a Japanese morphological analysis corps.[4]

- Initial annotation: Six annotators, the authors and three university students, annotated all the documents with NEs. Each document was annotated by only a member.

- Modification: Four of the annotators checked all the annotated documents again and modified annotation errors. Annotation disagreements are resolved based on discussion of annotators.

- Packaging : We prepared a package only including annotated tags with the positions in each documents. Users having BCCWJ can reproduce the BCCWJ Basic NE corpus with the package.

Table 2 shows the number of documents and NE tags of each genre in BCCWJ Basic NE corpus. For comparing purpose, the statistics of IREX data. The number of documents of BCCWJ Basic NE corpus is more than the sum of the number of the IREX evaluation data: GENERAL data, ARREST DATA. In addition, BCCWJ Basic NE corpus includes documents other than newspapers such as Yahoo! Chiebukuro and White Paper.

Table 3 shows the statistics of BCCWJ Basic NE corpus. Table 4 shows the percentage of each NE in a genre. We see from these statistics that BCCWJ Basic NE corpus has different property compared IREX. For example, we see that Yahoo! Chiebukuro and White Paper include more ARTIFACT than newspapers and Magazine includes more PERSON than the other genres.

4 Example Uses of BCCWJ Basic NE corpus

This section describes some example uses of BCCWJ Basic NE corpus.

4.1 Evaluation of an NE recognizer

We evaluated KNP that extracts the eight types of NEs listed in Table 1 based on the IREX definition. KNP is one of the freely available state of the art NE recognizers. We used Japanese morphological analyzer JUMAN version 7.01 [5] as a morphological analyzer of KNP version 4.12 [6].

Table 5 shows accuracy of KNP on BCCWJ Basic NE corpus. KNP was evaluated with Recall, Precision and F-measure:

- Recall = NUM / (the number of correct NEs)

- Precision = NUM / (the number of words and word chunks recognized as NEs by KNP)

---

[3]We referred the annotation guideline careted by IREX committee: https://nlp.cs.nyu.edu/irex/NE/df990214.txt . This site is only Japanese.

[4]http://plata.ar.media.kyoto-u.ac.jp/mori/research/ NLR/JDC/ClassA-1.list

[5]http://nlp.ist.i.kyoto-u.ac.jp/index.php?JUMAN
[6]http://nlp.ist.i.kyoto-u.ac.jp/index.php?KNP

BCCWJ		
Genre	the number of documents	the number of NEs
Yahoo! Chiebukuro (OC)	74	175
White Paper (OW)	8	656
Yahoo! Blog (OY)	34	307
Books (PB)	5	399
Magazines (PM)	2	319
Newspapers (PN)	13	705
Total	136	2,561 (2,464)

IREX		
Genre	the number of documents	the number of NEs
CRL	1174	19,262
DRY	36	832
NET	46	973
AT	23	466
AR	20	397
GE	72	1,667
Total	1,371	23,597 (22,822)

Table 2: The number of NEs in BCCWJ Basic NE corpus and the IREX data set. The documents of NEs for IREX data is the number of news articles. IREX data set consists of the following data created from Mainichi Shimbun news articles: CRL_NE_DATA.idx (CRL), DRYRUN03.idx (DRY), NEtraining981031.idx (NET), ARREST_TRAIN.idx (AT), ARREST01.idx (AR), GENERAL03.idx (GE). The numbers between parentheses in Total columns indicate the number of NEs excluding OPTIONAL.

- F-measure = 2 × Recall × Precision / (Recall + Precision)

where NUM is the number of correct NEs recognized by KNP.

Compared with Newspapers, KNP showed lower performance on Yahoo! Chiebukuro and Yahoo! Blog. One of the reasons seems that KNP was trained with IREX CRL data that consists of news articles. Another reason is Yahoo! Chiebukuro and Yahoo! Blog includes more abbreviations and colloquial expressions than newspapers. Furthermore, KNP also showed lower performance on White Paper even if White Paper documents were written language. One of the reasons seems that White Paper includes more ARTIFACT NEs than Newspapers The accuracy of KNP for ARTIFACT was lower than the other NEs on Newspapers.

From this evaluation, we see that we can evaluate NE recognizers with different perspective by using different genres of documents.

4.2 The Other Expected Use

We also expect that BCCWJ Basic NE corpus contributes to the following research.

- NE recognition for colloquial expressions: Yahoo! Blog contributes to NE recognition researches for colloquial expressions because Yahoo! Blog includes more colloquial expressions than Newspapers and White Paper

- Domain Adaptation: BCCWJ Basic NE corpus includes six genres of documents, therefore, we expect BCCWJ Basic NE corpus is useful for the research of domain adaptation (Daumé III, 2007).

- Revision learning for NE recognition: We also have uploaded not only latest annotation but also older versions of NE annotation results. Therefore, we can use the corpus as an error detection research or revision learning like Japanese morphological analysis (Nakagawa et al., 2002).

- Comparison of annotation performance on different genres of documents: We can use

BCCWJ

Genre	ART	DATE	LOC	MON	OPT	ORG	PERC	PERS	TIME
OC	54	19	57	9	8	19	0	6	3
OW	163	129	140	9	39	128	33	15	0
OY	25	60	52	7	9	61	11	79	3
PB	29	50	87	0	24	26	6	169	8
PM	13	42	32	5	4	17	1	203	2
PN	24	165	188	59	13	118	38	78	22
Total	308	465	557	89	97	369	89	550	37

IREX

Data	ART	DATE	LOC	MON	OPT	ORG	PERC	PERS	TIME
CRL	747	3567	5463	390	585	3676	492	3840	502
DRY	42	110	192	33	42	214	6	169	24
NET	67	137	255	32	47	270	19	138	8
AT	11	69	165	19	7	80	3	94	18
AR	13	72	106	8	8	74	0	97	19
GE	49	277	416	15	86	389	21	355	59
Total	929	4232	6597	497	775	4703	541	4693	630

Table 3: The number of NEs in BCCWJ Basic NE corpus. ART, LOC, MON, OPT, ORG, PERC and PERS indicate ARTIFACT, LOCATION, MONEY, OPTIONAL, ORGANIZATION, PERCENT and PERSON, respectively. The others are same as ones in Table 2.

this corpus for evaluating annotation performance and annotation methods on different genres of documents. One of the examples is described in (Komiya et al., 2016). The paper compared the following two methods to annotate a corpus via non-expert annotators for named entity (NE) recognition task. The first one is an annotation method by revising the results of an existing NE recognizer. The other is an annotation method by hand from the beginning.

5 Conclusion

This paper introduced a Japanese Named Entity (NE) corpus of various genres called BCCWJ Basic NE corpus. We annotated 136 documents in the BCCWJ with the eight types of NE tags defined by IREX. Users having BCCWJ can reproduce use the corpus by using the annotation information of the corpus distributed at a web site. Users having BCCWJ can reproduce use the corpus by using the annotation information of the corpus distributed at the following web site: https:// sites.google.com/site/projectnextnlpne/en/ .

Acknowledgments

We appreciate Ai Hirata, Maiko Yamazaki and Masaaki Ichihara for their help of building this corpus.

References

Hal Daumé III. 2007. Frustratingly easy domain adaptation. In *Proc. of ACL'07*.

Masatsugu Hangyo, Daisuke Kawahara, and Sadao Kurohashi. 2012. Building a diverse document leads corpus annotated with semantic relations. pages 535–544.

IREX Committee. 1999. *Proc. of the IREX workshop*.

Kanako Komiya, Masaya Suzuki, Tomoya Iwakura, Minoru Sasaki, and Hiroyuki Shinno. 2016. Comparison of annotating methods for named entity corpora. In *Proc. of LAW-X*.

Kikuo Maekawa, Makoto Yamazaki, Takehiko Maruyama, Masaya Yamaguchi, Hideki Ogura, Wakako Kashino, Toshinobu Ogiso, Hanae Koiso, and Yasuharu Den. 2010. Design, compilation, and preliminary analyses of balanced corpus of contemporary written japanese. In *Proceedings of the International Conference on Language Resources and Evaluation, LREC 2010, 17-23 May 2010, Valletta, Malta*.

BCCWJ

Genre	ART	DATE	LOC	MON	OPT	ORG	PERC	PERS	TIME
OC	30.86%	10.86%	32.57%	5.14%	4.57%	10.86%	0%	3.43%	1.71%
OW	24.85%	19.66%	21.34%	1.37%	5.95%	19.51%	5.03%	2.29%	0%
OY	8.14%	19.54%	16.94%	2.28%	2.93%	19.87%	3.58%	25.74%	0.98%
PB	7.27%	12.53%	21.80%	0%	6.02%	6.52%	1.50%	42.35%	2.01%
PM	4.08%	13.17%	10.03%	1.57%	1.25%	5.33%	0.31%	63.63%	0.63%
PN	3.40%	23.40%	26.68%	8.37%	1.84%	16.74%	5.39%	11.06%	3.12%

IREX

Genre	ART	DATE	LOC	MON	OPT	ORG	PERC	PERS	TIME
CRL	3.88%	18.52%	28.36%	2.02%	3.04%	19.08%	2.55%	19.94%	2.61%
DRY	5.05%	13.22%	23.08%	3.97%	5.05%	25.72%	0.72%	20.31%	2.88%
NET	6.89%	14.08%	26.21%	3.29%	4.83%	27.75%	1.95%	14.18%	0.82%
AT	2.36%	14.81%	35.41%	4.08%	1.50%	17.17%	0.64%	20.17%	3.86%
AR	3.27%	18.14%	26.69%	2.02%	2.02%	18.64%	0%	24.43%	4.79%
GE	2.94%	16.62%	24.95%	0.90%	5.16%	23.33%	1.26%	21.30%	3.54%

Table 4: The percentage of each NE in a genre. The meanings of items are same as ones in Table 2.

Tetsuji Nakagawa, Taku Kudo, and Yuji Matsumoto. 2002. Revision learning and its application to part-of-speech tagging. In *Proc. of ACL'02*, pages 497–504.

Satoshi Sekine, Kiyoshi Sudo, and Chikashi Nobata. 2002. Extended named entity hierarchy. In *Proc. of LREC'02*.

Erik F. Tjong Kim Sang and Fien De Meulder. 2003. Introduction to the conll-2003 shared task: Language-independent named entity recognition. In *Proc. of CoNLL'03*, pages 142–147.

R. Weischedel and A. Brunstein. 2005. Bbn pronoun coreference and entity type corpus. linguistic data consortium.

NE / Genre	Yahoo! Chiebukuro	White Paper
ARTIFACT	12.70 (7.41, 44.44)	45.69 (32.52, 76.81)
DATE	68.42 (68.42, 68.42)	77.52 (77.52, 77.52)
LOCATION	82.69 (75.44, 91.49)	86.47 (82.14, 91.27)
MONEY	100.00 (100.00, 100.00)	88.89 (88.89, 88.89)
ORGANIZATION	33.33 (26.32, 45.45)	70.83 (79.69, 63.75)
PERCENT	0 (0, 0)	96.88 (93.94, 100.00)
PERSON	33.33 (50.00, 25.00)	59.57 (93.33, 43.75)
Total	56.20 (46.11, 71.96)	72.12 (68.56, 76.08)

NE / Genre	Yahoo! Blog	Books
ARTIFACT	10.53 (8.00, 15.38)	48.78 (34.48, 83.33)
DATE	71.58 (56.67, 97.14)	51.69 (46.00, 58.97)
LOCATION	68.00 (65.38, 70.83)	57.99 (56.32, 59.76)
ORGANIZATION	50.00 (42.62, 60.47)	39.13 (34.62, 45.00)
PERCENT	95.24 (90.91, 100.00)	60.00 (50.00, 75.00)
PERSON	68.75 (69.62, 67.90)	72.67 (66.86, 79.58)
TIME	50.00 (33.33, 100.00)	80.00 (75.00, 85.71)
Total	63.06 (56.71, 71.01)	62.56 (56.80, 69.61)

NE / Genre	Magazines	Newspapers
ARTIFACT	72.73 (61.54, 88.89)	37.50 (37.50, 37.50)
DATE	86.08 (80.95, 91.89)	86.24 (85.45, 87.04)
LOCATION	28.07 (50.00, 19.51)	86.11 (82.01, 90.64)
MONEY	100.00 (100.00, 100.00)	94.12 (94.92, 93.33)
ORGANIZATION	66.67 (64.71, 68.75)	70.05 (64.41, 76.77)
PERCENT	100.00 (100.00, 100.00)	93.15 (89.47, 97.14)
PERSON	62.82 (53.69, 75.69)	87.34 (88.46, 86.25)
TIME	50.00 (50.00, 50.00)	72.73 (57.14, 100.00)
Total	60.56 (58.73, 62.50)	82.70 (79.77, 85.85)

Table 5: Accuracy of KNP on BCCWJ Basic NE corpus. The value indicates F-measure (Recall, Precision).

SOME LINGUISTIC ISSUES IN THE MACHINE TRANSLITERATION OF CHINESE, JAPANESE, AND ARABIC NAMES

Keynote address at 6th NEWS Named Entities Workshop
Jack Halpern
CEO, The CJK Dictionary Institute, Niiza, Japan

ABSTRACT

The romanization of non-Latin scripts is a complex computational task that is highly language dependent. This presentation will focus on three of the most challenging non-Latin scripts: Chinese, Japanese, and Arabic (CJA).

Much progress has been made in personal name machine-transliteration methodologies, as documented in the various NEWS reports over the last several years. Such techniques as phrase-based SMT, RNN-based LM and CRF have emerged, leading to gradual improvements in accuracy scores. But methodology is only one aspect of the problem. Equally important is the high level of ambiguity of the CJA scripts, which poses special challenges to named entity extraction and machine transliteration. These difficulties are exacerbated by the lack of comprehensive proper noun dictionaries, the multiplicity of ambiguous transcription schemes, and orthographic variation.

This presentation will clear up the differences between three basic concepts -- transliteration, transcription, and romanization -- that are a source of much confusion, even among computational linguists, and will focus on (1) the major linguistics issues, that is, the special characteristics of the CJA scripts that impact machine transliteration, and (2) the important role played by lexical resources such as personal name dictionaries.

A major issue in romanizing Simplified Chinese (SC) is the one-to-many ambiguity of many characters (*polyphones*), such as /lè/ and /yuè/ for 乐. To disambiguate accurately, the names must be looked up in word-level (not character-level) name mapping tables. This is complicated by (1) the presence of orthographic variants in traditional Chinese (TC), and (2) the need to for cross-script conversion between (SC) and (TC), Transcription into Chinese is even more ambiguous, since some phonemes can correspond to dozens of characters.

A major characteristic of Japanese, a highly agglutinative language, is the presence of countless orthographic variants. The four Japanese scripts interact in a complex way, resulting in *okurigana* variants (取り扱い, 取扱い, 取扱 etc. for /toriatsukai/), cross-script variants (猫, ねこ, ネコ for /neko/), kanji variants (大幅 and 大巾 for /oohaba/), kana variants (ユーザー and ユーザ for /yuuza(a)/), and more. Another issue is the numerous *kun* and *nanori* readings (some kanji have dozens) and the various romanization systems in current use, such as the Hepburn, Kunrei and hybrid systems.

Proceedings of the Sixth Named Entity Workshop, joint with 54th ACL, pages 47–48,
Berlin, Germany, August 12, 2016. ©2016 Association for Computational Linguistics

The Arabic script poses a different set of challenges to developers of NLP tools in general, and to machine transliteration of names in particular. This includes but is not limited to a high level of morphological and orthographical ambiguity, many ambiguous transcription schemes, and name variant expansion. For example, the string كاتب can represent distinct words such as /kaatib/, /kaataba/ and /kaatiba/, while long /aa/ can be written as ا, ى and آ. Automatically romanizing unvocalized Arabic without resorting to mapping tables is a complex task fraught with pitfalls.

These linguistic and orthographic difficulties are exacerbated by the lack of good lexical resources, especially of comprehensive personal name mapping tables. We will introduce several large-scale CJA name databases designed to support accurate romanization, transcription, and cross-script conversion (a subset of which has been used in the NEWS shared tasks over the last few years) and explain how these resources can be used to enhance the accuracy of name transliteration systems.

Whitepaper of NEWS 2016 Shared Task on Machine Transliteration[*]

Xiangyu Duan[*], Min Zhang[*], Haizhou Li[†], Rafael E. Banchs[†], A Kumaran[‡]

[*]Soochow University, China 215006
{xiangyuduan,minzhang}@suda.edu.cn

[†]Institute for Infocomm Research, A*STAR, Singapore 138632
{hli,rembanchs}@i2r.a-star.edu.sg

[‡]Multilingual Systems Research, Microsoft Research India
A.Kumaran@microsoft.com

Abstract

Transliteration is defined as phonetic translation of names across languages. Transliteration of Named Entities (NEs) is necessary in many applications, such as machine translation, corpus alignment, cross-language IR, information extraction and automatic lexicon acquisition. All such systems call for high-performance transliteration, which is the focus of shared task in the NEWS 2016 workshop. The objective of the shared task is to promote machine transliteration research by providing a common benchmarking platform for the community to evaluate the state-of-the-art technologies.

1 Task Description

The task is to develop machine transliteration system in one or more of the specified language pairs being considered for the task. Each language pair consists of a source and a target language. The training and development data sets released for each language pair are to be used for developing a transliteration system in whatever way that the participants find appropriate. At the evaluation time, a test set of source names only would be released, on which the participants are expected to produce a ranked list of transliteration candidates in another language (i.e. n-best transliterations), and this will be evaluated using common metrics. For every language pair the participants must submit at least one run that uses only the data provided by the NEWS workshop organisers in a given language pair (designated as "standard" run, primary submission). Users may submit more "stanrard" runs. They may also submit several "non-standard" runs for each language pair that use other data than those provided by the NEWS 2016

workshop; such runs would be evaluated and reported separately.

2 Important Dates

Research paper submission deadline	16 May 2016
Shared task	
Registration opens	29 Feb 2016
Registration closes	22 April 2016
Training/Development data release	29 Feb 2016
Test data release	25 April 2016
Results Submission Due	2 May 2016
Results Announcement	6 May 2016
Task (short) Papers Due	16 May 2016
For all submissions	
Acceptance Notification	13 June 2016
Camera-Ready Copy Deadline	20 June 2016
Workshop Date	12 Aug 2016

3 Participation

1. Registration (29 Feb 2016)

   (a) NEWS Shared Task opens for registration.

   (b) Prospective participants are to register to the NEWS Workshop homepage.

2. Training & Development Data (29 Feb 2016)

   (a) Registered participants are to obtain training and development data from the Shared Task organiser and/or the designated copyright owners of databases.

   (b) All registered participants are required to participate in the evaluation of at least one language pair, submit the results and a short paper and attend the workshop at ACL 2016.

3. Test data (25 April 2016)

---

[*]http://translit.i2r.a-star.edu.sg/news2016/

Proceedings of the Sixth Named Entity Workshop, joint with 54th ACL, pages 49–57,
Berlin, Germany, August 12, 2016. ©2016 Association for Computational Linguistics

(a) The test data would be released on 25 April 2016, and the participants have a maximum of 7 days to submit their results in the expected format.

(b) One "standard" run must be submitted from every group on a given language pair. Additional "standard" runs may be submitted, up to 4 "standard" runs in total. However, the participants must indicate one of the submitted "standard" runs as the "primary submission". The primary submission will be used for the performance summary. In addition to the "standard" runs, more "non-standard" runs may be submitted. In total, maximum 8 runs (up to 4 "standard" runs plus up to 4 "non-standard" runs) can be submitted from each group on a registered language pair. The definition of "standard" and "non-standard" runs is in Section 5.

(c) Any runs that are "non-standard" must be tagged as such.

(d) The test set is a list of names in source language only. Every group will produce and submit a ranked list of transliteration candidates in another language for each given name in the test set. Please note that this shared task is a "transliteration generation" task, i.e., given a name in a source language one is supposed to generate one or more transliterations in a target language. It is not the task of "transliteration discovery", i.e., given a name in the source language and a set of names in the target language evaluate how to find the appropriate names from the target set that are transliterations of the given source name.

4. Results (6 May 2016)

(a) On 6 May 2016, the evaluation results would be announced and will be made available on the Workshop website.

(b) Note that only the scores (in respective metrics) of the participating systems on each language pairs would be published, and no explicit ranking of the participating systems would be published.

(c) Note that this is a shared evaluation task and not a competition; the results are meant to be used to evaluate systems on common data set with common metrics, and not to rank the participating systems. While the participants can cite the performance of their systems (scores on metrics) from the workshop report, they should not use any ranking information in their publications.

(d) Furthermore, all participants should agree not to reveal identities of other participants in any of their publications unless you get permission from the other respective participants. By default, all participants remain anonymous in published results, unless they indicate otherwise at the time of uploading their results. Note that the results of all systems will be published, but the identities of those participants that choose not to disclose their identity to other participants will be masked. As a result, in this case, your organisation name will still appear in the web site as one of participants, but it will not be linked explicitly to your results.

5. Short Papers on Task (16 May 2016)

(a) Each submitting site is required to submit a 4-page system paper (short paper) for its submissions, including their approach, data used and the results on either test set or development set or by n-fold cross validation on training set.

(b) The review of the system papers will be done to improve paper quality and readability and make sure the authors' ideas and methods can be understood by the workshop participants. We are aiming at accepting all system papers, and selected ones will be presented orally in the NEWS 2016 workshop.

(c) All registered participants are required to register and attend the workshop to introduce your work.

(d) All paper submission and review will be managed electronically through https://www.softconf.com/acl2016/news2016/.

4   Language Pairs

The tasks are to transliterate personal names or place names from a source to a target language as summarised in Table 1. NEWS 2016 Shared Task offers 14 evaluation subtasks, among them ChEn and ThEn are the back-transliteration of EnCh and EnTh tasks respectively.   NEWS 2016 releases training, development and testing data for each of the language pairs. NEWS 2016 continues all language pairs that were evaluated in NEWS 2011, 2012 and 2015. In such cases, the training, development and test data in the release of NEWS 2016 are the same as those in NEWS 2015.

Please note that in order to have an accurate study of the research progress of machine transliteration technology, different from previous practice, the test/reference sets of NEWS 2011 are not released to the research community. Instead, we use the test sets of NEWS 2011 as progress test sets in NEWS 2016. NEWS 2016 participants are requested to submit results on the NEWS 2016 progress test sets (i.e., NEWS 2011 test sets). By doing so, we would like to do comparison studies by comparing the NEWS 2016 and NEWS 2011 results on the progress test sets and comparing the NEWS 2016 and the previous years' results on the test sets. We hope that we can have some insightful research findings in the progress studies.

The names given in the training sets for Chinese, Japanese, Korean, Thai and Persian languages are Western names and their respective transliterations; the Japanese Name (in English) → Japanese Kanji data set consists only of native Japanese names; the Arabic data set consists only of native Arabic names. The Indic data set (Hindi, Tamil, Kannada, Bangla) consists of a mix of Indian and Western names.

Examples of transliteration:

English → Chinese
> Timothy → 蒂莫西

English → Japanese Katakana
> Harrington → ハリントン

English → Korean Hangul
> Bennett → 베넷

Japanese name in English → Japanese Kanji
> Akihiro → 秋宏

English → Hindi
> San Francisco → सैन फ़्रान्सस्सिको

English → Tamil
> London → லண்டன்

English → Kannada
> Tokyo → ಟೋಕ್ಯೊ

Arabic → Arabic name in English
> خالد → Khalid

5   Standard Databases

Training Data (Parallel)
> Paired names between source and target languages; size 7K – 37K.
> Training Data is used for training a basic transliteration system.

Development Data (Parallel)
> Paired names between source and target languages; size 1K – 2.8K.
> Development Data is in addition to the Training data, which is used for system fine-tuning of parameters in case of need. Participants are allowed to use it as part of training data.

Testing Data
> Source names only; size 1K – 2K.
> This is a held-out set, which would be used for evaluating the quality of the transliterations.

Progress Testing Data
> Source names only; size 0.6K – 2.6K.
> This is the NEWS 2011 test set, it is held-out for progress study.

1. Participants will need to obtain licenses from the respective copyright owners and/or agree to the terms and conditions of use that are given on the downloading website (Li et al., 2004; MSRI, 2010; CJKI, 2010). NEWS 2016 will provide the contact details of each individual database. The data would be provided in Unicode UTF-8 encoding, in XML format; the results are expected to be submitted in UTF-8 encoding in XML format. The XML formats details are available in Appendix A.

2. The data are provided in 3 sets as described above.

3. Name pairs are distributed as-is, as provided by the respective creators.

Name origin	Source script	Target script	Data Owner	Data Size				Task ID
				Train	Dev	Progress Test	2016 Test	
Western	English	Chinese	Institute for Infocomm Research	37K	2.8K	2K	1K	EnCh
Western	Chinese	English	Institute for Infocomm Research	28K	2.7K	2.2K	1K	ChEn
Western	English	Korean Hangul	CJK Institute	7K	1K	609	1K	EnKo
Western	English	Japanese Katakana	CJK Institute	26K	2K	1.8K	1K	EnJa
Japanese	English	Japanese Kanji	CJK Institute	10K	2K	571	1K	JnJk
Arabic	Arabic	English	CJK Institute	27K	2.5K	2.6K	1K	ArEn
Mixed	English	Hindi	Microsoft Research India	12K	1K	1K	1K	EnHi
Mixed	English	Tamil	Microsoft Research India	10K	1K	1K	1K	EnTa
Mixed	English	Kannada	Microsoft Research India	10K	1K	1K	1K	EnKa
Mixed	English	Bangla	Microsoft Research India	13K	1K	1K	1K	EnBa
Western	English	Thai	NECTEC	27K	2K	2K	1K	EnTh
Western	Thai	English	NECTEC	25K	2K	1.9K	1K	ThEn
Western	English	Persian	Sarvnaz Karimi / RMIT	10K	2K	2K	1K	EnPe
Western	English	Hebrew	Microsoft Research India	9.5K	1K	1K	1K	EnHe

Table 1: Source and target languages for the shared task on transliteration.

(a) While the databases are mostly manually checked, there may be still inconsistency (that is, non-standard usage, region-specific usage, errors, etc.) or incompleteness (that is, not all right variations may be covered).

(b) The participants may use any method to further clean up the data provided.

  i. If they are cleaned up manually, we appeal that such data be provided back to the organisers for redistribution to all the participating groups in that language pair; such sharing benefits all participants, and further ensures that the evaluation provides normalisation with respect to data quality.

  ii. If automatic cleanup were used, such cleanup would be considered a part of the system fielded, and hence not required to be shared with all participants.

4. *Standard Runs* We expect that the participants to use only the data (parallel names) provided by the Shared Task for transliteration task for a "standard" run to ensure a fair evaluation. One such run (using only the data provided by the shared task) is mandatory for all participants for a given language pair that they participate in.

5. *Non-standard Runs* If more data (either parallel names data or monolingual data) were used, then all such runs using extra data must be marked as "non-standard". For such "non-standard" runs, it is required to disclose the size and characteristics of the data used in the system paper.

6. A participant may submit a maximum of 8 runs for a given language pair (including the mandatory 1 "standard" run marked as "primary submission").

6 Paper Format

Paper submissions to NEWS 2016 should follow the ACL 2016 paper submission policy, including paper format, blind review policy and title and author format convention. Full papers (research paper) are in two-column format without exceeding eight (8) pages of content plus two (2) extra page for references and short papers (task paper) are also in two-column format without exceeding four (4) pages content plus two (2) extra page for references. Submission must conform to the official ACL 2016 style guidelines. For details, please refer to the ACL 2016 website[2].

7 Evaluation Metrics

We plan to measure the quality of the transliteration task using the following 4 metrics. We accept up to 10 output candidates in a ranked list for each input entry.

Since a given source name may have multiple correct target transliterations, all these alternatives are treated equally in the evaluation. That is, any of these alternatives are considered as a correct

---

[2]http://www.ACL2016.org/

transliteration, and the first correct transliteration in the ranked list is accepted as a correct hit.

The following notation is further assumed:

N : Total number of names (source words) in the test set

n_i : Number of reference transliterations for i-th name in the test set ($n_i \geq 1$)

$r_{i,j}$: j-th reference transliteration for i-th name in the test set

$c_{i,k}$: k-th candidate transliteration (system output) for i-th name in the test set ($1 \leq k \leq 10$)

K_i : Number of candidate transliterations produced by a transliteration system

1. Word Accuracy in Top-1 (ACC) Also known as Word Error Rate, it measures correctness of the first transliteration candidate in the candidate list produced by a transliteration system. $ACC = 1$ means that all top candidates are correct transliterations i.e. they match one of the references, and $ACC = 0$ means that none of the top candidates are correct.

$$ACC = \frac{1}{N} \sum_{i=1}^{N} \left\{ \begin{array}{l} 1 \text{ if } \exists\, r_{i,j} : r_{i,j} = c_{i,1}; \\ 0 \text{ otherwise} \end{array} \right\} \tag{1}$$

2. Fuzziness in Top-1 (Mean F-score) The mean F-score measures how different, on average, the top transliteration candidate is from its closest reference. F-score for each source word is a function of Precision and Recall and equals 1 when the top candidate matches one of the references, and 0 when there are no common characters between the candidate and any of the references.

Precision and Recall are calculated based on the length of the Longest Common Subsequence between a candidate and a reference:

$$LCS(c, r) = \frac{1}{2} \left(|c| + |r| - ED(c, r) \right) \tag{2}$$

where ED is the edit distance and $|x|$ is the length of x. For example, the longest common subsequence between "abcd" and "afcde" is "acd" and its length is 3. The best matching reference, that is, the reference for which the edit distance has the minimum, is taken for calculation. If the best matching reference is given by

$$r_{i,m} = \arg\min_{j} \left(ED(c_{i,1}, r_{i,j}) \right) \tag{3}$$

then Recall, Precision and F-score for i-th word are calculated as

$$R_i = \frac{LCS(c_{i,1}, r_{i,m})}{|r_{i,m}|} \tag{4}$$

$$P_i = \frac{LCS(c_{i,1}, r_{i,m})}{|c_{i,1}|} \tag{5}$$

$$F_i = 2\frac{R_i \times P_i}{R_i + P_i} \tag{6}$$

- The length is computed in distinct Unicode characters.

- No distinction is made on different character types of a language (e.g., vowel vs. consonants vs. combining diereses' etc.)

3. Mean Reciprocal Rank (MRR) Measures traditional MRR *for any right answer* produced by the system, from among the candidates. $1/MRR$ tells approximately the average rank of the correct transliteration. MRR closer to 1 implies that the correct answer is mostly produced close to the top of the n-best lists.

$$RR_i = \left\{ \begin{array}{l} \min_j \frac{1}{j} \text{ if } \exists\, r_{i,j}, c_{i,k} : r_{i,j} = c_{i,k}; \\ 0 \text{ otherwise} \end{array} \right\} \tag{7}$$

$$MRR = \frac{1}{N} \sum_{i=1}^{N} RR_i \tag{8}$$

4. MAP$_{ref}$ Measures tightly the precision in the n-best candidates for i-th source name, for which reference transliterations are available. If all of the references are produced, then the MAP is 1. Let's denote the number of correct candidates for the i-th source word in k-best list as $num(i, k)$. MAP$_{ref}$ is then given by

$$MAP_{ref} = \frac{1}{N} \sum_{i}^{N} \frac{1}{n_i} \left(\sum_{k=1}^{n_i} num(i, k) \right) \tag{9}$$

8 Contact Us

If you have any questions about this share task and the database, please email to

Dr. Rafael E. Banchs

Institute for Infocomm Research (I^{2}R), A*STAR

1 Fusionopolis Way

#08-05 South Tower, Connexis

Singapore 138632

rembanchs@i2r.a-star.edu.sg

Dr. Min Zhang
Soochow University
China 215006
zhangminmt@hotmail.com

References

[CJKI2010] CJKI. 2010. CJK Institute. http://www.cjk.org/.

[Li et al.2004] Haizhou Li, Min Zhang, and Jian Su. 2004. A joint source-channel model for machine transliteration. In *Proc. 42nd ACL Annual Meeting*, pages 159–166, Barcelona, Spain.

[MSRI2010] MSRI. 2010. Microsoft Research India. http://research.microsoft.com/india.

A Training/Development Data

- File Naming Conventions:
  ```
  NEWS12_train_XXYY_nnnn.xml
  NEWS12_dev_XXYY_nnnn.xml
  NEWS12_test_XXYY_nnnn.xml
  NEWS11_test_XXYY_nnnn.xml
  (progress test sets)
  ```

  - XX: Source Language
  - YY: Target Language
  - nnnn: size of parallel/monolingual names ("25K", "10000", etc)

- File formats:
  All data will be made available in XML formats (Figure 1).

- Data Encoding Formats:
  The data will be in Unicode UTF-8 encoding files without byte-order mark, and in the XML format specified.

B Submission of Results

- File Naming Conventions:
  You can give your files any name you like. During submission online you will need to indicate whether this submission belongs to a "standard" or "non-standard" run, and if it is a "standard" run, whether it is the primary submission.

- File formats:
  All data will be made available in XML formats (Figure 2).

- Data Encoding Formats:
  The results are expected to be submitted in UTF-8 encoded files without byte-order mark only, and in the XML format specified.

```xml
<?xml version="1.0" encoding="UTF-8"?>

<TransliterationCorpus
    CorpusID = "NEWS2012-Train-EnHi-25K"
    SourceLang = "English"
    TargetLang = "Hindi"
    CorpusType = "Train|Dev"
    CorpusSize = "25000"
    CorpusFormat = "UTF8">

    <Name ID=" 1" >
        <SourceName>eeeeee1</SourceName>
        <TargetName ID="1">hhhhhh1_1</TargetName>
            <TargetName ID="2">hhhhhh1_2</TargetName>
        ...
        <TargetName ID="n">hhhhhh1_n</TargetName>
    </Name>
    <Name ID=" 2" >
        <SourceName>eeeeee2</SourceName>
        <TargetName ID="1">hhhhhh2_1</TargetName>
        <TargetName ID="2">hhhhhh2_2</TargetName>
        ...
        <TargetName ID="m">hhhhhh2_m</TargetName>
    </Name>
    ...
    <!-- rest of the names to follow -->
    ...
</TransliterationCorpus>
```

Figure 1: File: NEWS2012_Train_EnHi_25K.xml

```xml
<?xml version="1.0" encoding="UTF-8"?>

<TransliterationTaskResults
    SourceLang = "English"
    TargetLang = "Hindi"
    GroupID = "Trans University"
    RunID = "1"
    RunType = "Standard"
    Comments = "HMM Run with params: alpha=0.8 beta=1.25">

    <Name ID="1">
        <SourceName>eeeeee1</SourceName>
        <TargetName ID="1">hhhhhh11</TargetName>
        <TargetName ID="2">hhhhhh12</TargetName>
        <TargetName ID="3">hhhhhh13</TargetName>
        ...
        <TargetName ID="10">hhhhhh110</TargetName>

        <!-- Participants to provide their
        top 10 candidate transliterations -->
    </Name>
    <Name ID="2">
        <SourceName>eeeeee2</SourceName>
        <TargetName ID="1">hhhhhh21</TargetName>
        <TargetName ID="2">hhhhhh22</TargetName>
        <TargetName ID="3">hhhhhh23</TargetName>
        ...
        <TargetName ID="10">hhhhhh110</TargetName>
        <!-- Participants to provide their
        top 10 candidate transliterations -->
    </Name>
    ...
    <!-- All names in test corpus to follow -->
    ...
</TransliterationTaskResults>
```

Figure 2: Example file: NEWS2012_EnHi_TUniv_01_StdRunHMMBased.xml

Report of NEWS 2016 Machine Transliteration Shared Task

Xiangyu Duan[2],Rafael E. Banchs[1], Min Zhang[2], Haizhou Li[1], A. Kumaran[3]

[1] Institute for Infocomm Research, A*STAR, Singapore 138632
{rembanchs,hli}@i2r.a-star.edu.sg

[2] Soochow University, China 215006
{xiangyuduan,minzhang}@suda.edu.cn

[3]Multilingual Systems Research, Microsoft Research India
a.kumaran@microsoft.com

Abstract

This report presents the results from the Machine Transliteration Shared Task conducted as part of The Sixth Named Entities Workshop (NEWS 2016) held at ACL 2016in Berlin, Germany. Similar to previous editions of NEWS Workshop, the Shared Task featured machine transliteration of proper names over 14 different language pairs, including 12 different languages and two different Japanese scripts.A total of 5 teams participated in the evaluation, submitting 255 standard and 19 non-standard runs, involving a diverse variety of transliteration methodologies. Four performance metrics were used to report the evaluation results. Once again, the NEWS shared task on machine transliteration has successfully achieved its objectives by providing a common ground for the research community to conduct comparative evaluations of state-of-the-art technologies that will benefit the future research and development in this area.

1   Introduction

Names play an important role in the performance of most Natural Language Processing (NLP) and Information Retrieval (IR) applications. They are also critical in cross-lingual applications such as Machine Translation (MT) and Cross-language Information Retrieval (CLIR), as it has been shown that system performance correlates positively with the quality of name conversion across languages (Demner-Fushman and Oard 2002, Mandl and Womser-Hacker 2005,Hermjakobet al. 2008, Udupa et al. 2009). Bilingual dictionaries constitute the traditional source of information for name conversion across languages, however they offer very limited support due to the fact that, in most languages, names are continuously emerging and evolving.

All of the above points to the critical need for robust Machine Transliteration methods and systems. During the last decade, significant efforts has been conducted by the research community to address the problem of machine transliteration (Knight and Graehl 1998, Meng et al. 2001, Li et al. 2004, Zelenko and Aone 2006, Sproat et al. 2006, Sherif and Kondrak 2007, Hermjakob et al. 2008, Al-Onaizan and Knight 2002,Goldwasser and Roth 2008, Goldberg and Elhadad 2008,Klementiev and Roth 2006, Oh and Choi 2002, Virga and Khudanpur 2003, Wan and Verspoor 1998, Kang and Choi 2000, Gao et al. 2004,Li et al. 2009a, Li et al. 2009b). These previous works fall into three main categories: grapheme-based, phoneme-based and hybrid methods. Graphemebased methods (Li et al. 2004) treat transliteration as a direct orthographic mapping and only uses orthography-related features while phoneme-based methods (Knight and Graehl 1998) make use of phonetic correspondences to generate the transliteration. The hybrid approach refers to the combination of several different models or knowledge sources to support the transliteration generation process.

The first machine transliteration shared task (Li et al. 2009b, Li et al. 2009a) was organized and conducted aspart of NEWS 2009 at ACL-IJCNLP 2009. It was the first time that common benchmarking data in diverse language pairs was provided for evaluating state-of-the-art machine transliteration. While the focus of the 2009 shared task was on establishing the quality metrics and on setting up a baselinefor transliteration quality based on those metrics, the 2010 shared task (Li et al. 2010a, Li et al. 2010b) focused on expanding the scope of the transliteration generation task to about a dozen languages and on exploring the quality of the task depending on the direction of transliteration. In NEWS 2011 (Zhang et al. 2011a, Zhang et al. 2011b),

Proceedings of the Sixth Named Entity Workshop, joint with 54th ACL, pages 58–72,
Berlin, Germany, August 12, 2016. ©2016 Association for Computational Linguistics

the focus was on significantly increasing the hand-crafted parallel corpora of named entities to include 14 different language pairs from 11 language families, and on making them available as the common dataset for the shared task. The NEWS 2016Shared Task on Transliteration has been a continued effort for evaluating machine transliteration performance over such a common dataset following the NEWS 2015 (Banchs, et al., 2015), NEWS 2012and 2011 shared tasks.

In thispaper, we presentin full detail the results of the NEWS 2016Machine Transliteration Shared Task. The rest of the paper is structured as follows. Section 2 provides as short review of the main characteristics of the machine transliteration task and the corpora used for it. Section 3 reviews the four metrics used for the evaluations. Section 4 reports specific details about participation in the 2016 edition of the shared task, and section 5 presents and discusses the evaluation results. Finally, section 6 presents our main conclusions and future plans.

2   Shared Task on Transliteration

Transliteration, sometimes also called Romanization, especially if Latin Scripts are used for target strings (Halpern 2007), deals with the conversion of names between two languages and/or script systems. Within the context of the Transliteration Shared Task, we are aiming not only at addressing the name conversion process but also its practical utility for downstream applications, such as MT and CLIR.

In this sense, we adopt the same definition of transliteration as proposed during the NEWS 2009 workshop (Li et al. 2009a). According to it, transliteration is understood as the "conversion of a given name in the source language (a text string in the source writing system or orthography) to a name in the target language (another text string in the target writing system or orthography" conditioned to the following specific requirements regarding the name representation in the target language:

- it is phonetically equivalent to the source name,
- it conforms to the phonology of the target language, and
- it matches the user intuition on its equivalence with respect to the source language name.

Following NEWS 2011, NEWS 2012 and NEWS2015, the three back-transliteration tasks are maintained. Back-transliteration attempts to restore transliterated names back into their original source language. For instance, the tasks for converting western names written in Chinese and Thai back into their original English spellings are considered. Similarly, a task for back-transliterating Romanized Japanese names into their original Kanji strings is considered too.

2.1   Shared Task Description

Following the tradition of NEWS workshop series, the shared task in NEWS 2016 consists of developing machine transliteration systems in one or more of the specified language pairs.Each language pair of the shared task consists of asource and a target language, implicitly specifyingthe transliteration direction. Training and developmentdata in each of the language pairs was made available to all registered participants for developing their transliteration systems.

At the evaluation time, a standard hand-crafted test set consisting of between 500 and 3,000source names (approximately 5-10% of the trainingdata size) was released, on which theparticipants were required to produce a ranked listof transliteration candidates in the target languagefor each source name. The system output istested against a reference set (which may includemultiple correct transliterations for some sourcenames), and the performance of a system is capturedin multiple metrics (defined in Section 3),each designed to capture a specific performancedimension.

For every language pair, each participant was requiredto submit at least one run (designated as a"standard" run) that uses only the data provided bythe NEWS workshop organizers in that languagepair; i.e. no other data or linguistic resources are allowed for standard runs. Thisensures parity between systems andenables meaningful comparison of performanceof various algorithmic approaches in a given languagepair. Participants were allowed to submitone or more standard runs for each task they participated in. If more thanone standard runs were submitted, it was required toname one of them as a "primary" run, which was the one used to compare results across different systems.

In addition, more than one "non-standard" runs could besubmitted for every language pair using either databeyond theone provided by the shared task organizers,any other available linguistic resources in a specific language pair, or both. This essentially enabled participants to demonstrate the limits of performance of theirsystems in a given language pair.

2.2 Shared Task Corpora

Two specific constraints were considered when selectinglanguages for the shared task: language diversityand data availability. To make the shared taskinteresting and to attract wider partic-ipation, it isimportant to ensure a reasonable variety amongthe languages in terms of linguistic diversity, orthographyand geography. Clearly, the ability ofprocuring and distributing a reasonably large (approximately10K paired names for training andtesting together) hand-crafted corpora consistingprimarily of paired names is critical for this process. Following NEWS 2015, the 14 tasks shown in Tables 1.a-ewere used (Li et al.2004, Kumaran and Kellner 2007, MSRI 2009,CJKI 2010).

The names given in the training sets for Chinese,Japanese, Korean, Thai, Persian and Hebrewlanguages are Western names and their respectivetransliterations; the Japanese Name (in English) → Japanese Kanji data set consists only of nativeJapanese names; the Arabic data set consists onlyof native Arabic names. The Indic data set (Hindi,Tamil, Kannada, Bangla) consists of a mix of Indianand Western names.

For all of the tasks chosen, we have been able to procure paired-name data between thesource and the target scripts and were able tomake them available to the participants. Forsome language pairs, such as the case of English-Chinese andEnglish-Thai, there are both transliteration and-back-transliteration tasks. Most of the tasks are justone-way transliteration, although Indian data setscontainsa mixture of names from both Indian andWestern origins.

3 Evaluation Metrics and Rationale

The participants have been asked to submit standard and, optionally, non-standard runs.One of the standard runs must be named as the primarysubmission, which was the one used for the performance summary.Each run must contain a ranked list of up toten candidate transliterations for each source name.The submitted results are compared to the groundtruth (reference transliterations) using four evaluationmetrics capturing different aspects of transliterationperformance. The four considered evaluation metrics are:

- Word Accuracy in Top-1 (ACC),
- Fuzziness in Top-1 (Mean F-score),
- Mean Reciprocal Rank (MRR), and
- Mean Average Precision (MAP_{ref}).

Task ID:EnCh			data size		
Origin	Source	Target	Train	Dev	Test
Western	English	Chinese	37K	2.8K	1.0K
Task ID: ChEn			data size		
Origin	Source	Target	Train	Dev	Test
Western	Chinese	English	28K	2.7K	1.0K

Table 1.a: Datasets provided by Institute for Infocomm Research, Singapore.

Task ID: EnKo			data size		
Origin	Source	Target	Train	Dev	Test
Western	English	Korean	7.0K	1.0K	1.0K
Task ID: EnJa			data size		
Origin	Source	Target	Train	Dev	Test
Western	English	Katakana	26K	2.0K	1.0K
Task ID: JnJk			data size		
Origin	Source	Target	Train	Dev	Test
Japanese	English	Kanji	10K	2.0K	1.0K
Task ID: ArEn			data size		
Origin	Source	Target	Train	Dev	Test
Arabic	Arabic	English	27K	2.5K	1.0K

Table 1.b: Datasets provided by the CJK Institute, Japan.

Task ID: EnHi			data size		
Origin	Source	Target	Train	Dev	Test
Mixed	English	Hindi	12K	1.0K	1.0K
Task ID: EnTa			data size		
Origin	Source	Target	Train	Dev	Test
Mixed	English	Tamil	10K	1.0K	1.0K
Task ID: EnKa			data size		
Origin	Source	Target	Train	Dev	Test
Mixed	English	Kannada	10K	1.0K	1.0K
Task ID: EnBa			data size		
Origin	Source	Target	Train	Dev	Test
Mixed	English	Bangla	13K	1.0K	1.0K
Task ID: EnHe			data size		
Origin	Source	Target	Train	Dev	Test
Western	English	Hebrew	9.5K	1.0K	1.0K

Table 1.c: Datasets provided by Microsoft Research India.

Task ID: EnTh			data size		
Origin	Source	Target	Train	Dev	Test
Western	English	Thai	27K	2.0K	1.0K
Task ID: ThEn			data size		
Origin	Source	Target	Train	Dev	Test
Western	Thai	English	25K	2.0K	1.0K

Table 1.d: Datasets provided by National Electronics and Computer Technology Center.

Task ID: EnPe			data size		
Origin	Source	Target	Train	Dev	Test
Western	English	Persian	10K	2.0K	1.0K

Table 1.e: Dataset provided bySarvnazKarimi / RMIT.

In the next subsections, we present a brief description of the four considered evaluation metrics. The following notation is further assumed:

- N : Total number of names (sourcewords) in the test set,
- n_i : Number of reference transliterationsfor i-th name in the test set ($n_i \geq 1$),
- $r_{i,j}$: j-th reference transliteration for i-thname in the test set,
- $c_{i,k}$: k-th candidate transliteration (systemoutput) for i-th name in the test set($1 \leq k \leq 10$),
- K_i : Number of candidate transliterationsproduced by a transliteration system.

3.1 Word Accuracy in Top-1 (ACC)

Also known as Word Error Rate, it measures correctnessof the first transliteration candidate in thecandidate list produced by a transliteration system.$ACC = 1$ means that all top candidates are correcttransliterations; i.e. they match one of the references,and $ACC = 0$ means that none of the topcandidates are correct.

$$ACC = \frac{1}{N}\sum_{i=1}^{N} \begin{cases} 1 \ if \ \exists r_{i,j} : r_{i,j} = c_{i,1} \ ; \\ 0 \ otherwise \end{cases} \quad (Eq.1)$$

3.2 Fuzziness in Top-1 (Mean F-score)

The Mean F-score measures how different, on average,the top transliteration candidate is from itsclosest reference. F-score for each source wordis a function of Precision and Recall and equals 1when the top candidate matches one of the references, and 0 when there are no common charactersbetween the candidate and any of the references.

Precision and Recall are calculated based onthe length of the Longest Common Subsequence(LCS) between a candidate and a reference:

$$LCS(c,r) = \frac{1}{2}\big(|c| + |r| - ED(c,r)\big) \quad (Eq.2)$$

whereED is the edit distance and $|x|$ is the lengthof x. For example, the longest common subsequencebetween "abcd" and "afcde" is "acd" andits length is 3. The best matching reference, i.e. the reference for which the edit distance hasthe minimum, is taken for calculation. If the best-matching reference is given by

$$r_{i,m} = \arg min_j \big(ED(c_{i,1}, r_{i,j})\big) \quad (Eq.3)$$

the Recall, Precision and F-score for the i-th word are calculated as:

$$R_i = \frac{LCS(c_{i,1}, r_{i,m})}{|r_{i,m}|} \quad (Eq.4)$$

$$P_i = \frac{LCS(c_{i,1}, r_{i,m})}{|c_{i,1}|} \quad (Eq.5)$$

$$F_i = 2\frac{R_i \times P_i}{R_i + P_i} \quad (Eq.6)$$

The lengths are computed with respect to distinct Unicode characters, and no distinctions are made for different character types of a language (e.g. vowel vs. consonant vs. combining diereses, etc.).

3.3 Mean Reciprocal Rank (MRR)

Measures traditional MRR for any right answerproduced by the system, from among the candidates.1/MRR tells approximately the averagerank of the correct transliteration. MRR closer to 1implies that the correct answer is mostly producedclose to the top of the n-best lists.

$$RR_i = \begin{cases} min_j \frac{1}{j} \ if \ \exists r_{i,j}, c_{i,k} : r_{i,j} = c_{i,k} \ ; \\ 0 \ otherwise \end{cases} \quad (Eq.7)$$

$$MRR = \frac{1}{N}\sum_{i=1}^{N} RR_i \quad (Eq.8)$$

3.4 Mean Average Precision (MAP$_{ref}$)

This metric measures tightly the precision in the n-best candidates for i-th source name, for which reference transliterations are available. If all of the referencesare produced, then the MAP is 1. If we denotethe number of correct candidates for the i-thsource word in k-best list as $num(i,k)$, thenMAP$_{ref}$is given by:

$$MAP_{ref} = \frac{1}{N}\sum_{i=1}^{N}\frac{1}{n_i}\Big(\sum_{k=1}^{n_i} num(i,k)\Big) \quad (Eq.9)$$

4 Participation in the Shared Task

A total of five teams from five different institutions participated in the NEWS 2016 Shared Task. More specifically, the participating teams were from National Institute of Information and Communications Technology (NICT), Qazvin Islamic Azad University (QIAU), University of Helsinki (UOH), Uppsala University (UPPS), Institute for Infocomm Research (I2R).

Teams were required to submit at least one standard run for every task they participated in, and for NEWS 2012/2015 test sets. They are set as the official NEWS 2016 evaluation set. In total, we received 31 standard and 2 non-standard runs for all test sets; i.e. 255 standard and 19 non-standard runs in total. Table 2 summarizes the number of standard runs, non-standard runs and teams participating per task.

Task	Std	Non	Teams Participating
EnCh	25	0	NICT,UPPS, QIAU, UOH
ChEn	27	2	NICT, UPPS, QIAU, UOH
EnKo	15	0	NICT
EnJa	15	0	NICT
JnJk	15	0	NICT
ArEn	0	0	
EnHi	19	0	NICT, QIAU, UOH
EnTa	17	0	NICT, QIAU
EnKa	17	0	NICT, QIAU
EnBa	20	0	NICT, QIAU, UOH
EnHe	24	2	NICT, QIAU, UOH
EnTh	22	0	NICT, QIAU, I2R
ThEn	16	0	NICT, QIAU
EnPe	23	15	NICT, QIAU, UOH
	255	19	

Table 2: Number of standard (Std) and non-standard (Non) runs submitted, and teams participating in each task.

As seen from the table, the most popular task continues to be the transliteration from English to Chinese and Chinese to English (Zhang et al. 2012), followed by English to Hindi etc. Non-standard runs were only submitted for 3 of the 14 tasks.

4.1 Shared Task on CodaLab

Different from previous years, in NEWS 2016 the Shared Task evaluation was run online by using the CodaLab platform (http://codalab.org/). CodaLab is a powerful online platform aiming at accelerating reproducible computational research. Two main functionalities are available at the CodaLab platform: worksheets, which allows for running reproducible experiments and creating executable papers; and competitions, which allows for participating and/or hosting competitions.

CodaLab's competitions allows for running competitions that involve either code submissions or data submissions. For the case of NEWS 2016 Shared Task on transliteration, two CodaLab competitions on the data submission modality were created: NEWS 2016 Standard submissions (https://competitions.codalab.org/ competitions/8991) and NEWS 2016 Non-standard submissions(https://competitions.codalab.org/ competitions/9021). In the standard submissions competition, participants were required to use only the training and development data provided by the Shared Task, while for the non-standard submissions competitions, in addition to the training and development data provided by the Shared Task, participants were welcomed to use external data, either parallel or monolingual. A total of 12 and 4 participants registered for the standard submissions and non-standard submissions competitions, respectively, but finally only five teams submitted results into the competitions.

Each competition was composed of 14 phases, each corresponding to one of the 14 transliteration tasks available in the Shared Task. All phases were run in parallel, meaning that each participant was able to submit results to any of the phases at any moment during the evaluation campaign, which ran from April 25th to May 3rd. During this period, participants were allowed to submit to each of the two competitions up to 3 results per day and per task, with an overall maximum of 15 submissions per task during the complete evaluation period. For each task they participated in, participants were allowed to post only one result in the corresponding leader-board. The leader-boards for both the standard submissions and non-standard submissions competitions are available at https://competitions.codalab.org/ competitions/8991#results and https:// competitions.codalab.org/competitions/9021#results, respectively.

4.2 Baseline System Results

Also different from previous years, in NEWS 2016 a baseline system was set up and baseline results were computed for all the 14 transliteration tasks available in the Shared Task. Baseline results were based on a simple MT implementation at the character level using MOSES. The baseline system was generously provided by UPC, Barcelona (Costa-jussa, 2016).

A summary of NEWS 2016 Shared Task results, including the MOSES-based baseline results, is available in the workshop's website at: http://workshop.colips.org/news2016/results.html.

5 Task Results and Analysis

Figure 1 summarizes the results of the NEWS 2016 Shared Task. In the figure, only F-scores over the NEWS 2015 evaluation test set (referred to as NEWS15/16) for all primary standard submissions are depicted. A total of 31 primary standard submissions were received.

As seen from the figure, with the exception of the English to Japanese Katakana, only transliteration tasks involving Arabic, Persian and the four considered Indian languages are consistently scored above 80%. For the rest of the languages, with the exception of Japanese Katakana and Hebrew, scores are consistently in the range from 60% to 80%. Notice also that, regardless the availability of training data, the English to Chinese transliteration task seems to be the more demanding one for state-of-the-art systems with respect to the considered metric.

Another interesting observation that can be derived from the figure, when looking to the language pairs English-Chinese and English-Thai, is that systems tend to perform slightly better for the case of back-transliteration tasks.

A much more comprehensive presentation of results for the NEWS 2016 Shared Task is provided in the Appendix at the end of this paper. There, resulting scores are reported for all received submissions, including standard and non-standard submissions and the four considered evaluation metrics. All results are presented in 14 tables, each of which reports the scores for one transliteration task over one test set. In the tables, all primary standard runs are highlighted in bold-italic fonts.

Regarding the systems participating in this year evaluation, two highest performance systems of the five participants submitted their system description papers, which are from NICT and UPPS. The NICT's system (Finch et al. 2016) applied neural network Ensembles, each of which explores the agreement of target-bidirectional sequence-to-sequence neural network model. The ensembles show great improvements over their NEWS 2015 results, which utilized a rescoring reranking function to ensemble attention-based neural network and traditional machine translation models.

The UPPS's system (Shao et al. 2016) implemented a neural network trained on unsupervised sub-units alignments. They used a convolutional neural network to encode character-level transliteration information and a recurrent neural network as stacking. Their decoding performance demonstrates that their proposed neural network significantly outperforms the baseline which is a character-level system trained by Moses.

As seen from the previous system descriptions, neural networks become more and more predominant in the state-of-the-art machine transliteration. Significant improvements are achieved by neural network ensembles, while single neural network also obtains better performance than traditional phrase-based machine translation systems. The simple ensemble method achieved the best performance across all 14 phases.

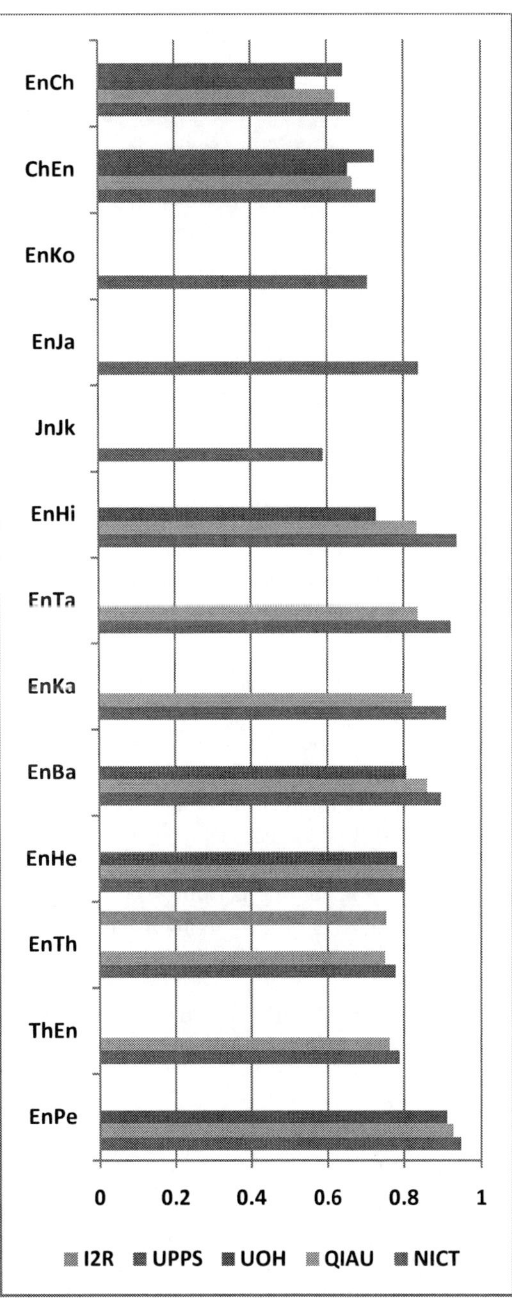

Figure 1: Mean F-scores (Top-1) on the evaluation test set (NEWS12/15) for all primary standard submissions and all transliteration tasks.

Finally, figure 2 compares, in terms of Mean F-scores, the best primary standard submissions in NEWS 2015 with the ones in NEWS 2016.

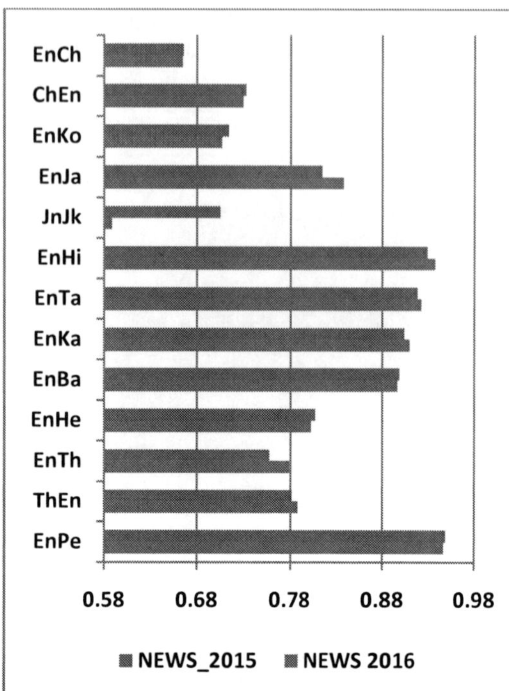

Figure 2: Mean F-scores (Top-1) on the evaluation test set (NEWS12/15) for the best primary standard submissions in 2012 and 2015.

As seen from the figure, in most of the considered transliteration tasks, some incremental improvements can be observed between the 2015 and 2016 shared tasks. The most significant improvements are in those tasks involving Japanese Katakana, Tamil, Kannada, and Thai.

Regarding the observed drops in performance, the most significant one is from JnJk. It is mainly due to that the specific participant NICT applied a totally different methodology compared to JnJk in 2015. As their system description paper points out, the drop is because the large vocabulary set on the target side that neural network hardly handles.

6   Conclusions

The Shared Task on Machine Transliteration in NEWS 2016 has shown, once again, that the research community has a continued interest in this area. This report summarizes the results of the NEWS 2016 Shared Task.

We are pleased to report a comprehensive set of machine transliteration approaches and their evaluation results over the evaluation test set, as well as two conditions: standard runs and non-standard runs.While the standard runs allow for conducting meaningful comparisons across different algorithms, the non-standard runs open up

more opportunities for exploiting a varietyof additional linguistic resources.

Five teams from five different institutions participated in the shared task. In total, we received 31 standard and 2 non-standard runs for each test set; i.e. 255 standard and 19 non-standard runs in total. Most of the current state-of-the-art in machine transliteration is represented in the systems that have participated in the shared task.

Encouraged by the continued success of the NEWS workshopseries, we plan to continue this event in the future to further promoting machine transliteration research and development.

Acknowledgments

The organizers of the NEWS 2016 Shared Task would like to thank the Institute for Infocomm Research (Singapore), Microsoft Research India, CJK Institute (Japan), National Electronics and Computer Technology Center (Thailand) and Sarvnaz Karim / RMIT for providing the corpora and technical support. Without those, the Shared Task would not be possible. We also want to thank all program committee members for their valuable comments that improved the quality of the shared task papers. Finally, we wish to thank all participants for their active participation, which have made again the NEWS Machine Transliteration Shared Task a successful one.

References

Y. Al-Onaizan, K. Knight. 2002. Machine transliteration of names in arabic text. In Proc. ACL-2002Workshop: Computational Apporaches to Semitic Languages, Philadelphia, PA, USA.

D. Bahdanau, K. Cho, Y. Bengio. 2014. Neural machine translation by jointly learning to align and translate. Cornell University Library, arXiv:1409.0473 [cs.CL]

R. Banchs; M. Zhang; X. Duan; H. Li; A. Kumaran. 2015. Report of NEWS 2015 Machine Transliteration Shared Task. Proceedings of the Fifth Named Entity Workshop, joint with 53rd Annual Meeting of the Association for Computational Linguistics, Beijing, China.

M. Bisani, H. Ney. 2008. Joint sequence models for grapheme-to-phoneme conversion. Speech Communication, 50(5):434–451.

CJKI. 2010. CJK Institute. http://www.cjk.org/.

M. Costa-juss`. 2016. Moses-based official baseline for NEWS 2016. Proceedings of the Sixth Named Entity Workshop, joint with 54th Annual Meeting of the Association for Computational Linguistics, Berlin, Germany.

D. Demner-Fushman, D.W. Oard. 2002. The effect of bilingual term list size on dictionary-based cross-language information retrieval. In Proc. 36-th Hawaii Int'l. Conf. System Sciences, volume 4, page 108.2.

A. Finch, P. Dixon, E. Sumita. 2012. Rescoring a phrase-based machine transliteration system with recurrent neural network language models. In Proceedings of the 4th Named Entity Workshop (NEWS) 2012, pages 47–51, Jeju, Korea, July.

A. Finch, L. Liu, X. Wang, E. Sumita. 2015.Neural Network Transduction Models in Transliteration Generation. In Proceedings of the 2015 Named Entities Workshop: Shared Task on Transliteration (NEWS 2015), Beijing, China.

A. Finch, L. Liu, X. Wang, E. Sumita. 2016. Target-Bidirectional Neural Models for Machine Transliteration. In Proceedings of the 2016 Named Entities Workshop: Shared Task on Transliteration (NEWS 2016), Berlin, German.

W. Gao, K.F. Wong, W. Lam. 2004. Phoneme-based transliteration of foreign names for OOV problem. In Proc. IJCNLP, pages 374–381, Sanya, Hainan, China.

Y. Goldberg, M. Elhadad. 2008. Identification of transliterated foreign words in Hebrew script. In Proc. CICLing, volume LNCS 4919, pages 466–477.

D. Goldwasser, D. Roth. 2008. Transliteration as constrained optimization. In Proc. EMNLP, pages 353–362.

J. Halpern. 2007. The challenges and pitfalls of Arabic romanization and arabization. In Proc. Workshop on Comp. Approaches to Arabic Scriptbased Lang.

U. Hermjakob, K. Knight, H. Daum. 2008. Name translation in statistical machine translation: Learning when to transliterate. In Proc. ACL, Columbus, OH, USA, June.

S. Jiampojamarn, G. Kondrak, T. Sherif. 2007. Applying many-to-many alignments and hidden markov models to letter-to-phoneme conversion. In proceedings of Human Language Technologies 2007: The Conference of the North American Chapter of the Association for Computational Linguistics; pages 372–379, Rochester, New York, April.

S. Jiampojamarn, A. Bhargava, Q. Dou, K. Dwyer, G. Kondrak. 2009. DirecTL: a language independent approach to transliteration. In Proceedings of the 2009 Named Entities Workshop: Shared Task on Transliteration (NEWS 2009), pages 28–31, Suntec, Singapore.

S. Jiampojamarn, C. Cherry, G. Kondrak. 2010. Integrating joint n-gram features into a discriminative training framework. In Proceedings of NAACL-2010, Los Angeles, CA, June.Association for Computational Linguistics.

B.J. Kang, K.S. Choi. 2000. English-Korean automatic transliteration/ backtransliteration system and character alignment. In Proc. ACL, pages 17–18, Hong Kong.

A. Klementiev, D. Roth. 2006. Weakly supervised named entity transliteration and discovery from multilingual comparable corpora. In Proc. 21st Int'l Conf Computational Linguistics and 44th Annual Meeting of ACL, pages 817–824, Sydney, Australia, July.

K. Knight, J. Graehl. 1998. Machine transliteration. Computational Linguistics, 24(4).

P. Koehn, H. Hoang, A. Birch, C. Callison-Burch, M. Federico, N. Bertoldi, B. Cowan, W. Shen, C. Moran, R. Zens, C. Dyer, O. Bojar, A. Constantin, E. Herbst. 2007. Moses: Open source toolkit for statistical machine translation. In Proceedings of the 45th Annual Meeting of the Association for Computational Linguistics Companion Volume Proceedings of the Demo and Poster Sessions, pages 177–180, Prague, Czech Republic.

A. Kumaran, T. Kellner. 2007. A generic framework for machine transliteration. In Proc. SIGIR, pages 721–722.

A. Kunchukuttan, P. Bhattacharyya. 2015. Data representation methods and use of mined corpora for Indian language transliteration. In Proceedings of the 2015 Named Entities Workshop: Shared Task on Transliteration (NEWS 2015), Beijing, China.

H. Li, M. Zhang, J. Su. 2004. A joint source-channel model for machine transliteration. In Proc. 42nd ACL Annual Meeting, pages 159–166, Barcelona, Spain.

H. Li, A. Kumaran, V. Pervouchine, M. Zhang. 2009a. Report of NEWS 2009 machine transliteration shared task. In Proc. Named Entities Workshop at ACL 2009.

H. Li, A. Kumaran, M. Zhang, V. Pervouchine. 2009b. ACL-IJCNLP 2009 Named Entities Workshop - Shared Task on Transliteration. In Proc. Named Entities Workshop at ACL 2009.

H. Li, A. Kumaran, M. Zhang, V. Pervouchine. 2010a. Report of news 2010 transliteration generation shared task. In Proc. Named Entities Workshop at ACL 2010.

H. Li, A. Kumaran, M. Zhang, V. Pervouchine. 2010b. Whitepaper of news 2010 shared task on transliteration generation. In Proc. Named Entities Workshop at ACL 2010.

T. Mandl, C. Womser-Hacker. 2005. The effect of named entities on effectiveness in cross-language information retrieval evaluation. In Proc. ACM Symp.Applied Comp., pages 1059–1064.

H.M. Meng, W.K. Lo, B. Chen, K. Tang. 2001. Generate phonetic cognates to handle name entities in English-Chinese cross-language spoken document retrieval. In Proc. ASRU.

MSRI. 2009. Microsoft Research India. http://research. microsoft.com/india.

G. Nicolai, B. Hauer, M. Salameh, A. St Arnaud, Y. Xu, L. Yao, G. Kondrak. 2015. Multiple System Combination for Transliteration. In Proceedings of the 2015 Named Entities Workshop: Shared Task on Transliteration (NEWS 2015), Beijing, China.

J.H. Oh, K.S. Choi. 2002. An English-Korean transliteration model using pronunciation and contextual rules. In Proc. COLING 2002, Taipei, Taiwan.

Y. Shao, J. Nivre. 2016. Applying Neural Networks to English-Chinese Named Entity Transliteration. In Proceedings of the 2016 Named Entities Workshop: Shared Task on Transliteration (NEWS 2016), Berlin, Germany.

T. Sherif, G. Kondrak. 2007. Substringbased transliteration. In Proc. 45th Annual Meeting of the ACL, pages 944–951, Prague, Czech Republic, June.

R. Sproat, T. Tao, C.X. Zhai. 2006. Named entity transliteration with comparable corpora. In Proc. 21st Int'l Conf Computational Linguistics and 44th Annual Meeting of ACL, pages 73–80, Sydney, Australia.

R. Udupa, K. Saravanan, A. Bakalov, A. Bhole. 2009. "They are out there, if you know where to look": Mining transliterations of OOV query terms for cross-language information retrieval. In LNCS: Advances in Information Retrieval, volume 5478, pages 437–448. Springer Berlin / Heidelberg.

P. Virga, S. Khudanpur. 2003. Transliteration of proper names in cross-lingual information retrieval. In Proc. ACL MLNER, Sapporo, Japan.

S. Wan, C.M. Verspoor. 1998. Automatic English-Chinese name transliteration for development of multilingual resources. In Proc. COLING, pages 1352–1356.

D. Wang, X. Yang, J. Xu, Y. Chen, N. Wang, B. Liu, J. Yang, Y. Zhang. 2015a. A Hybrid Transliteration Model for Chinese/English Named Entities — BJTU-NLP Report for the 5th Named Entities Workshop. In Proceedings of the 2015 Named Entities Workshop: Shared Task on Transliteration (NEWS 2015), Beijing, China.

Y.C. Wang, C.K. Wu, R.T.H. Tsai. 2015b. NCU IISR English-Korean and English-Chinese Named Entity Transliteration Using Different Grapheme Segmentation Approaches. In Proceedings of the 2015 Named Entities Workshop: Shared Task on Transliteration (NEWS 2015), Beijing, China.

D. Zelenko, C. Aone. 2006. Discriminative methods for transliteration. In Proc. EMNLP, pages 612–617, Sydney, Australia, July.

M. Zhang, A. Kumaran, H. Li. 2011a. Whitepaper of news 2011 shared task on machine transliteration. In Proc. Named Entities Workshop at IJCNLP 2011.

M. Zhang, H. Li, A. Kumaran, M. Liu. 2011b. Report of news 2011 machine transliteration shared task. In Proc. Named Entities Workshop at IJCNLP 2011.

M. Zhang, H. Li, A. Kumaran, M. Liu. 2012. Report of NEWS 2012 Machine Transliteration Shared Task. Proceedings of the 50th Annual Meeting of the Association for Computational Linguistics, pages 10–20, Jeju, Republic of Korea.

Appendix: Evaluation Results

Team	Accuracy	F-score	MRR	MAP$_{ref}$
UPPS	0.3353 (1)	0.6759 (1)	0.3963 (4)	0.3233 (1)
NICT	0.3165 (2)	0.6643 (2)	0.4130 (1)	0.3086 (2)
NICT	0.3145 (3)	0.6629 (3)	0.4100 (2)	0.3056 (3)
NICT	0.3085 (4)	0.6604 (5)	0.4037 (3)	0.2995 (4)
NICT	0.3056 (5)	0.6467 (14)	0.3938 (5)	0.2946 (6)
NICT	0.3006 (6)	0.6606 (4)	0.3920 (6)	0.2949 (5)
NICT	0.2996 (7)	0.6489 (13)	0.3871 (7)	0.2924 (7)
NICT	0.2986 (8)	0.6533 (10)	0.3739 (11)	0.2901 (8)
NICT	0.2966 (9)	0.6540 (9)	0.3814 (8)	0.2873 (10)
NICT	0.2966 (9)	0.6567 (6)	0.3799 (9)	0.2858 (11)
NICT	0.2966 (9)	0.6564 (7)	0.3787 (10)	0.2887 (9)
NICT	0.2877 (10)	0.6509 (11)	0.3698 (14)	0.2798 (13)
NICT	0.2867 (11)	0.6546 (8)	0.3724 (12)	0.2761 (14)
NICT	0.2837 (12)	0.6491 (12)	0.3711 (13)	0.2750 (15)
UPPS	0.2808 (13)	0.6434 (15)	0.3007 (18)	0.2812 (12)
NICT	0.2768 (14)	0.6421 (16)	0.3591 (15)	0.2680 (16)
NICT	0.2728 (15)	0.6373 (17)	0.3583 (16)	0.2653 (17)
QIAU	0.2659 (16)	0.6227 (18)	0.3185 (17)	0.2549 (18)
UOH	0.1062 (17)	0.5160 (19)	0.1062 (19)	0.1014 (19)
UOH	0.0992 (18)	0.5021 (20)	0.0992 (20)	0.0945 (20)
UOH	0.0010 (19)	0.1989 (21)	0.0010 (21)	0.0010 (21)
UOH	0.0010 (19)	0.1989 (21)	0.0010 (21)	0.0010 (21)
QIAU	0.0000 (20)	0.0871 (22)	0.0000 (22)	0.0000 (22)

Table 1: Results for the English to Chinese transliteration task (EnCh) on Evaluation Test.

Team	Accuracy	F-score	MRR	MAP$_{ref}$
NICT	0.2139 (1)	0.7292 (4)	0.3026 (2)	0.2119 (1)
NICT	0.2110 (2)	0.7309 (2)	0.3016 (3)	0.2091 (2)
NICT	0.2100 (3)	0.7308 (3)	0.3038 (1)	0.2076 (3)
NICT	0.2012 (4)	0.7212 (6)	0.2774 (6)	0.1978 (4)
NICT	0.2002 (5)	0.7182 (7)	0.2798 (5)	0.1978 (5)
UPPS	0.1992 (6)	0.7524 (1)	0.2810 (4)	0.1947 (6)
NICT	0.1904 (7)	0.7067 (14)	0.2679 (9)	0.1866 (7)
NICT	0.1884 (8)	0.7150 (10)	0.2718 (7)	0.1831 (10)
NICT	0.1884 (8)	0.7165 (8)	0.2693 (8)	0.1854 (8)
NICT	0.1865 (9)	0.7164 (9)	0.2678 (10)	0.1851 (9)
NICT	0.1835 (10)	0.7103 (13)	0.2658 (11)	0.1813 (11)
NICT	0.1825 (11)	0.7120 (12)	0.2606 (12)	0.1800 (12)
NICT	0.1766 (12)	0.7122 (11)	0.2550 (14)	0.1735 (13)
NICT	0.1747 (13)	0.7065 (15)	0.2560 (13)	0.1717 (14)
NICT	0.1698 (14)	0.6987 (17)	0.2481 (15)	0.1679 (15)
UPPS	0.1619 (15)	0.7253 (5)	0.1816 (17)	0.1620 (16)
UPPS	0.1619 (15)	0.7253 (5)	0.1816 (17)	0.1620 (16)
NICT	0.1600 (16)	0.6989 (16)	0.2450 (16)	0.1578 (17)

UOH	0.1099 (17)	0.6687 (18)	0.1099 (19)	0.1066 (18)
UOH	0.0854 (18)	0.6500 (20)	0.0854 (20)	0.0825 (20)
QIAU	0.0834 (19)	0.6564 (19)	0.1425 (18)	0.0830 (19)
QIAU	0.0834 (19)	0.6564 (19)	0.1425 (18)	0.0830 (19)
UOH	0.0000 (20)	0.4770 (21)	0.0000 (21)	0.0000 (21)
UOH	0.0000 (20)	0.4770 (21)	0.0000 (21)	0.0000 (21)

Table 2: Results for the Chinese to English transliteration task (ChEn) on Evaluation Test.

Team	Accuracy	F-score	MRR	MAP$_{ref}$
NICT	0.1869 (1)	0.7784 (1)	0.2789 (1)	0.1869 (1)
NICT	0.1837 (2)	0.7759 (2)	0.2782 (2)	0.1837 (2)
NICT	0.1788 (3)	0.7735 (3)	0.2740 (3)	0.1788 (3)
NICT	0.1756 (4)	0.7626 (6)	0.2575 (4)	0.1756 (4)
NICT	0.1707 (5)	0.7675 (4)	0.2501 (6)	0.1707 (5)
NICT	0.1691 (6)	0.7557 (8)	0.2384 (8)	0.1691 (6)
NICT	0.1650 (7)	0.7635 (5)	0.2501 (5)	0.1650 (7)
NICT	0.1586 (8)	0.7567 (7)	0.2439 (7)	0.1586 (8)
NICT	0.1570 (9)	0.7550 (10)	0.2382 (10)	0.1570 (9)
NICT	0.1570 (9)	0.7550 (9)	0.2382 (9)	0.1570 (9)
NICT	0.1553 (10)	0.7550 (11)	0.2372 (11)	0.1553 (10)
I2R	0.1553 (10)	0.7537 (13)	0.1561 (17)	0.1553 (10)
NICT	0.1537 (11)	0.7516 (15)	0.2297 (14)	0.1537 (11)
NICT	0.1529 (12)	0.7542 (12)	0.2346 (12)	0.1529 (12)
NICT	0.1456 (13)	0.7497 (17)	0.2229 (15)	0.1456 (13)
QIAU	0.1456 (13)	0.7514 (16)	0.2181 (16)	0.1456 (13)
NICT	0.1448 (14)	0.7522 (14)	0.2314 (13)	0.1448 (14)
I2R	0.1440 (15)	0.7491 (18)	0.1448 (18)	0.1440 (15)
I2R	0.1173 (16)	0.7452 (19)	0.1173 (19)	0.1173 (16)
I2R	0.0631 (17)	0.6687 (20)	0.0631 (20)	0.0631 (17)
I2R	0.0437 (18)	0.6572 (21)	0.0437 (21)	0.0437 (18)

Table 3: Results for the English to Thai transliteration task (EnTh) on Evaluation Test.

Team	Accuracy	F-score	MRR	MAP$_{ref}$
NICT	0.1958 (1)	0.7881 (2)	0.2914 (1)	0.1958 (1)
NICT	0.1942 (2)	0.7897 (1)	0.2885 (2)	0.1942 (2)
NICT	0.1942 (2)	0.7871 (3)	0.2853 (3)	0.1942 (2)
NICT	0.1699 (3)	0.7739 (4)	0.2531 (4)	0.1699 (3)
NICT	0.1667 (4)	0.7692 (6)	0.2424 (5)	0.1667 (4)
NICT	0.1594 (5)	0.7681 (8)	0.2413 (6)	0.1594 (5)
NICT	0.1537 (6)	0.7659 (11)	0.2326 (10)	0.1537 (6)
NICT	0.1529 (7)	0.7657 (13)	0.2325 (11)	0.1529 (7)
NICT	0.1521 (8)	0.7681 (9)	0.2412 (7)	0.1521 (8)
NICT	0.1521 (8)	0.7691 (7)	0.2354 (8)	0.1521 (8)
NICT	0.1513 (9)	0.7630 (15)	0.2207 (15)	0.1513 (9)
NICT	0.1497 (10)	0.7652 (14)	0.2245 (13)	0.1497 (10)
NICT	0.1472 (11)	0.7673 (10)	0.2280 (12)	0.1472 (11)
NICT	0.1464 (12)	0.7657 (12)	0.2221 (14)	0.1464 (12)

| NICT | 0.1456 (13) | 0.7715 (5) | 0.2330 (9) | 0.1456 (13) |
| QIAU | 0.1286 (14) | 0.7624 (16) | 0.1966 (16) | 0.1286 (14) |

Table 4: Results for the Thai to English transliteration task (ThEn) on Evaluation Test.

Team	Accuracy	F-score	MRR	MAP$_{ref}$
NICT	0.6958 (1)	0.9466 (2)	0.7952 (1)	0.6799 (1)
NICT	0.6939 (2)	0.9481 (1)	0.7921 (2)	0.6787 (2)
NICT	0.6910 (3)	0.9455 (3)	0.7908 (3)	0.6747 (3)
NICT	0.6555 (4)	0.9388 (5)	0.7594 (6)	0.6388 (5)
NICT	0.6545 (5)	0.9391 (4)	0.7597 (5)	0.6402 (4)
NICT	0.6488 (6)	0.9373 (6)	0.7627 (4)	0.6326 (6)
NICT	0.6449 (7)	0.9363 (8)	0.7562 (8)	0.6288 (7)
NICT	0.6401 (8)	0.9363 (7)	0.7564 (7)	0.6245 (9)
NICT	0.6382 (9)	0.9356 (10)	0.7473 (10)	0.6199 (10)
NICT	0.6382 (9)	0.9357 (9)	0.7531 (9)	0.6273 (8)
NICT	0.6296 (10)	0.9351 (11)	0.7463 (11)	0.6153 (11)
NICT	0.6276 (11)	0.9328 (12)	0.7385 (12)	0.6137 (12)
NICT	0.5912 (12)	0.9299 (13)	0.7174 (13)	0.5763 (13)
QIAU	0.5816 (13)	0.9267 (14)	0.7116 (14)	0.5673 (15)
QIAU	0.5816 (13)	0.9267 (14)	0.7116 (14)	0.5673 (15)
NICT	0.5797 (14)	0.9235 (16)	0.7012 (16)	0.5710 (14)
QIAU	0.5758 (15)	0.9261 (15)	0.7090 (15)	0.5633 (16)
UOH	0.5077 (16)	0.9103 (18)	0.5077 (17)	0.4718 (17)
UOH	0.5029 (17)	0.9104 (17)	0.5029 (18)	0.4678 (18)
UOH	0.3369 (18)	0.8711 (19)	0.3369 (19)	0.3138 (19)
NICT	0.0000 (19)	0.0000 (20)	0.0000 (20)	0.0000 (20)

Table 5: Results for the English to Persian transliteration task (EnPe) on Evaluation Test.

Team	Accuracy	F-score	MRR	MAP$_{ref}$
NICT	0.7150 (1)	0.9371 (1)	0.7814 (2)	0.7091 (1)
NICT	0.7130 (2)	0.9339 (3)	0.7821 (1)	0.7086 (2)
NICT	0.7090 (3)	0.9344 (2)	0.7807 (3)	0.7044 (3)
NICT	0.6460 (4)	0.9174 (5)	0.7223 (7)	0.6425 (4)
NICT	0.6450 (5)	0.9164 (7)	0.7249 (5)	0.6382 (5)
NICT	0.6410 (6)	0.9162 (8)	0.7265 (4)	0.6356 (6)
NICT	0.6370 (7)	0.9160 (9)	0.7172 (9)	0.6306 (7)
NICT	0.6370 (7)	0.9191 (4)	0.7241 (6)	0.6305 (8)
NICT	0.6310 (8)	0.9164 (6)	0.7181 (8)	0.6264 (9)
NICT	0.6270 (9)	0.9103 (11)	0.7125 (10)	0.6229 (10)
NICT	0.6230 (10)	0.9138 (10)	0.7116 (11)	0.6190 (11)
NICT	0.6120 (11)	0.9090 (13)	0.7066 (12)	0.6085 (12)
NICT	0.6080 (12)	0.9098 (12)	0.6994 (14)	0.6037 (13)
NICT	0.6050 (13)	0.9057 (14)	0.6995 (13)	0.5992 (14)
NICT	0.5780 (14)	0.9055 (15)	0.6814 (15)	0.5724 (15)
QIAU	0.3480 (15)	0.8349 (16)	0.4745 (16)	0.3434 (16)
UOH	0.1090 (16)	0.7292 (17)	0.1090 (17)	0.1061 (17)
UOH	0.0300 (17)	0.6073 (18)	0.0300 (18)	0.0285 (18)

| QIAU | 0.0000 (18) | 0.2553 (19) | 0.0002 (19) | 0.0000 (19) |

Table 6: Results for the English to Hindi transliteration task (EnHi) on Evaluation Test.

Team	Accuracy	F-score	MRR	MAP$_{ref}$
NICT	0.6290 (1)	0.9216 (1)	0.7171 (1)	0.6280 (1)
NICT	0.6200 (2)	0.9204 (2)	0.7148 (2)	0.6190 (2)
NICT	0.6130 (3)	0.9186 (3)	0.7120 (3)	0.6120 (3)
NICT	0.5910 (4)	0.9101 (4)	0.6795 (4)	0.5902 (4)
NICT	0.5890 (5)	0.9091 (5)	0.6778 (5)	0.5882 (5)
NICT	0.5720 (6)	0.9074 (6)	0.6674 (7)	0.5712 (6)
NICT	0.5690 (7)	0.9048 (7)	0.6725 (6)	0.5685 (7)
NICT	0.5640 (8)	0.9029 (8)	0.6597 (8)	0.5642 (8)
NICT	0.5450 (9)	0.8999 (10)	0.6500 (9)	0.5445 (9)
NICT	0.5390 (10)	0.8986 (11)	0.6399 (11)	0.5388 (10)
NICT	0.5380 (11)	0.9011 (9)	0.6465 (10)	0.5370 (11)
NICT	0.5180 (12)	0.8949 (12)	0.6248 (12)	0.5182 (12)
NICT	0.4980 (13)	0.8883 (13)	0.6081 (14)	0.4972 (13)
NICT	0.4950 (14)	0.8880 (14)	0.6099 (13)	0.4940 (14)
NICT	0.4460 (15)	0.8824 (15)	0.5731 (15)	0.4452 (15)
QIAU	0.3240 (16)	0.8369 (16)	0.4461 (16)	0.3235 (16)
QIAU	0.0000 (17)	0.3623 (17)	0.0001 (17)	0.0000 (17)

Table 7: Results for the English to Tamil transliteration task (EnTa) on Evaluation Test.

Team	Accuracy	F-score	MRR	MAP$_{ref}$
NICT	0.5830 (1)	0.9089 (1)	0.6815 (1)	0.5819 (1)
NICT	0.5700 (2)	0.9076 (2)	0.6752 (2)	0.5689 (2)
NICT	0.5650 (3)	0.9053 (3)	0.6703 (3)	0.5639 (3)
NICT	0.5250 (4)	0.8894 (6)	0.6159 (6)	0.5246 (4)
NICT	0.5230 (5)	0.8902 (4)	0.6229 (4)	0.5219 (5)
NICT	0.5190 (6)	0.8900 (5)	0.6170 (5)	0.5185 (6)
NICT	0.5130 (7)	0.8832 (11)	0.6134 (8)	0.5128 (7)
NICT	0.5070 (8)	0.8861 (10)	0.6078 (10)	0.5061 (9)
NICT	0.5070 (8)	0.8892 (7)	0.6129 (9)	0.5059 (10)
NICT	0.5070 (8)	0.8867 (9)	0.6156 (7)	0.5066 (8)
NICT	0.5020 (9)	0.8870 (8)	0.6022 (11)	0.5011 (11)
NICT	0.4790 (10)	0.8801 (12)	0.5864 (12)	0.4792 (12)
NICT	0.4320 (11)	0.8695 (13)	0.5569 (13)	0.4314 (13)
NICT	0.4280 (12)	0.8635 (14)	0.5479 (14)	0.4280 (14)
NICT	0.3990 (13)	0.8509 (15)	0.5001 (15)	0.3988 (15)
QIAU	0.2860 (14)	0.8224 (16)	0.4019 (16)	0.2856 (16)
QIAU	0.0000 (15)	0.3288 (17)	0.0000 (17)	0.0000 (17)

Table 8: Results for the English to Kannada transliteration task (EnKa) on Evaluation Test.

Team	Accuracy	F-score	MRR	MAP$_{ref}$
NICT	0.4980 (1)	0.8955 (3)	0.6266 (1)	0.4978 (1)
NICT	0.4980 (1)	0.8975 (1)	0.6243 (2)	0.4965 (2)
NICT	0.4890 (2)	0.8963 (2)	0.6167 (3)	0.4873 (3)
NICT	0.4320 (3)	0.8799 (4)	0.5537 (4)	0.4301 (4)

NICT	0.4260 (4)	0.8786 (6)	0.5413 (7)	0.4255 (5)
NICT	0.4250 (5)	0.8763 (7)	0.5519 (5)	0.4226 (7)
NICT	0.4250 (5)	0.8798 (5)	0.5481 (6)	0.4240 (6)
NICT	0.4210 (6)	0.8748 (8)	0.5399 (8)	0.4192 (8)
NICT	0.4170 (7)	0.8695 (14)	0.5327 (11)	0.4138 (11)
NICT	0.4160 (8)	0.8710 (12)	0.5320 (13)	0.4150 (9)
NICT	0.4160 (8)	0.8734 (9)	0.5388 (9)	0.4147 (10)
NICT	0.4130 (9)	0.8729 (10)	0.5374 (10)	0.4115 (12)
NICT	0.4110 (10)	0.8723 (11)	0.5309 (14)	0.4099 (13)
NICT	0.4100 (11)	0.8696 (13)	0.5327 (12)	0.4088 (14)
NICT	0.3980 (12)	0.8686 (15)	0.5238 (15)	0.3965 (15)
QIAU	0.3460 (13)	0.8600 (16)	0.4737 (16)	0.3438 (16)
UOH	0.1990 (14)	0.8063 (17)	0.1990 (17)	0.1969 (17)
UOH	0.1830 (15)	0.7958 (18)	0.1830 (18)	0.1814 (18)
UOH	0.1070 (16)	0.7379 (19)	0.1070 (19)	0.1059 (19)
QIAU	0.0000 (17)	0.2583 (20)	0.0000 (20)	0.0000 (20)

Table 9: Results for the English to Bangla transliteration task (EnBa) on Evaluation Test.

Team	Accuracy	F-score	MRR	MAP_{ref}
NICT	0.1891 (1)	0.8031 (1)	0.2679 (3)	0.1877 (1)
NICT	0.1882 (2)	0.8023 (3)	0.2695 (2)	0.1868 (2)
NICT	0.1845 (3)	0.8029 (2)	0.2700 (1)	0.1832 (3)
NICT	0.1809 (4)	0.7952 (5)	0.2516 (5)	0.1802 (4)
NICT	0.1800 (5)	0.7951 (7)	0.2506 (6)	0.1793 (5)
NICT	0.1800 (5)	0.7902 (11)	0.2577 (4)	0.1784 (6)
NICT	0.1755 (6)	0.7926 (8)	0.2448 (11)	0.1739 (7)
NICT	0.1745 (7)	0.7896 (14)	0.2460 (9)	0.1731 (8)
NICT	0.1745 (7)	0.7888 (15)	0.2453 (10)	0.1730 (9)
NICT	0.1736 (8)	0.7918 (10)	0.2447 (12)	0.1720 (10)
NICT	0.1727 (9)	0.7902 (12)	0.2485 (7)	0.1711 (11)
NICT	0.1718 (10)	0.7879 (16)	0.2469 (8)	0.1702 (12)
NICT	0.1709 (11)	0.7919 (9)	0.2443 (13)	0.1693 (13)
NICT	0.1709 (11)	0.7831 (17)	0.2404 (15)	0.1693 (13)
NICT	0.1682 (12)	0.7897 (13)	0.2432 (14)	0.1664 (14)
QIAU	0.1591 (13)	0.7976 (4)	0.2377 (16)	0.1582 (15)
UOH	0.1482 (14)	0.7817 (19)	0.1482 (17)	0.1466 (16)
UOH	0.1445 (15)	0.7951 (6)	0.1445 (18)	0.1436 (17)
UOH	0.1382 (16)	0.7828 (18)	0.1382 (19)	0.1366 (18)
UOH	0.1355 (17)	0.7746 (20)	0.1355 (20)	0.1339 (19)

Table 10: Results for the English to Hebrew transliteration task (EnHe) on Evaluation Test.

Team	Accuracy	F-score	MRR	MAP_{ref}
NICT	0.3524 (1)	0.7067 (1)	0.4509 (2)	0.3526 (1)
NICT	0.3505 (2)	0.7032 (2)	0.4518 (1)	0.3507 (2)
NICT	0.3476 (3)	0.7022 (3)	0.4505 (3)	0.3476 (3)
NICT	0.3229 (4)	0.6885 (4)	0.4090 (4)	0.3226 (4)
NICT	0.3181 (5)	0.6762 (7)	0.4057 (5)	0.3190 (5)

NICT	0.3133 (6)	0.6794 (5)	0.4023 (7)	0.3136 (6)
NICT	0.3124 (7)	0.6735 (10)	0.4042 (6)	0.3126 (7)
NICT	0.3067 (8)	0.6782 (6)	0.3998 (8)	0.3064 (9)
NICT	0.3067 (8)	0.6747 (9)	0.3987 (9)	0.3064 (9)
NICT	0.3067 (8)	0.6659 (12)	0.3946 (11)	0.3069 (8)
NICT	0.3000 (9)	0.6647 (13)	0.3875 (13)	0.2998 (10)
NICT	0.2971 (10)	0.6702 (11)	0.3912 (12)	0.2974 (12)
NICT	0.2971 (10)	0.6624 (15)	0.3815 (14)	0.2979 (11)
NICT	0.2952 (11)	0.6749 (8)	0.3958 (10)	0.2955 (13)
NICT	0.2895 (12)	0.6631 (14)	0.3794 (15)	0.2890 (14)

Table 11: Results for the English to Korean transliteration task (EnKo) on Evaluation Test.

Team	Accuracy	F-score	MRR	MAP$_{ref}$
NICT	0.4647 (1)	0.8386 (1)	0.5916 (1)	0.4637 (1)
NICT	0.4637 (2)	0.8386 (2)	0.5902 (2)	0.4627 (2)
NICT	0.4608 (3)	0.8359 (3)	0.5830 (3)	0.4601 (3)
NICT	0.4182 (4)	0.8160 (5)	0.5434 (4)	0.4177 (4)
NICT	0.4153 (5)	0.8210 (4)	0.5400 (5)	0.4148 (5)
NICT	0.4105 (6)	0.8141 (8)	0.5346 (6)	0.4090 (6)
NICT	0.4066 (7)	0.8155 (6)	0.5259 (9)	0.4056 (7)
NICT	0.4008 (8)	0.8154 (7)	0.5252 (10)	0.3998 (8)
NICT	0.3988 (9)	0.8110 (9)	0.5143 (12)	0.3969 (9)
NICT	0.3979 (10)	0.8099 (11)	0.5270 (8)	0.3964 (11)
NICT	0.3979 (10)	0.8102 (10)	0.5340 (7)	0.3967 (10)
NICT	0.3950 (11)	0.8043 (13)	0.5210 (11)	0.3921 (12)
NICT	0.3843 (12)	0.8029 (14)	0.5129 (13)	0.3824 (13)
NICT	0.3775 (13)	0.8067 (12)	0.4982 (14)	0.3768 (14)
NICT	0.0000 (14)	0.0000 (15)	0.0000 (15)	0.0000 (15)

Table 12: Results for the English to Japanese (Kantakana) transliteration task (EnJa) on Evaluation Test.

Team	Accuracy	F-score	MRR	MAP$_{ref}$
NICT	0.3269 (1)	0.5886 (1)	0.3883 (3)	0.2465 (3)
NICT	0.3251 (2)	0.5867 (2)	0.3911 (1)	0.2489 (2)
NICT	0.3233 (3)	0.5845 (3)	0.3900 (2)	0.2490 (1)
NICT	0.3169 (4)	0.5782 (4)	0.3821 (4)	0.2459 (4)
NICT	0.3160 (5)	0.5698 (5)	0.3724 (6)	0.2385 (5)
NICT	0.3096 (6)	0.5651 (7)	0.3774 (5)	0.2375 (6)
NICT	0.3087 (7)	0.5625 (9)	0.3684 (8)	0.2333 (7)
NICT	0.3041 (8)	0.5545 (12)	0.3689 (7)	0.2263 (8)
NICT	0.3023 (9)	0.5665 (6)	0.3577 (11)	0.2257 (9)
NICT	0.2986 (10)	0.5626 (8)	0.3585 (10)	0.2250 (10)
NICT	0.2950 (11)	0.5562 (10)	0.3606 (9)	0.2249 (11)
NICT	0.2922 (12)	0.5561 (11)	0.3532 (12)	0.2198 (13)
NICT	0.2895 (13)	0.5520 (13)	0.3511 (13)	0.2209 (12)
NICT	0.2868 (14)	0.5506 (14)	0.3474 (14)	0.2195 (14)
NICT	0.2804 (15)	0.5417 (15)	0.3396 (15)	0.2120 (15)

Table 13: Results for the English to Japanese (Kanji) transliteration task (JnJk) on Evaluation Test.

Applying Neural Networks to English-Chinese Named Entity Transliteration

Yan Shao, Joakim Nivre

Department of Linguistics and Philology

Uppsala University

{yan.shao, joakim.nivre}@lingfil.uu.se

Abstract

This paper presents the machine transliteration systems that we employ for our participation in the NEWS 2016 machine transliteration shared task. Based on the prevalent deep learning models developed for general sequence processing tasks, we use convolutional neural networks to extract character level information from the transliteration units and stack a simple recurrent neural network on top for sequence processing. The systems are applied to the standard runs for both English to Chinese and Chinese to English transliteration tasks. Our systems achieve competitive results according to the official evaluation.

1 Introduction

Transliteration is the process of transcribing the source characters ideally accurately as well as unambiguously into a target language that uses a different writing system while preserving the pronunciation. Machine transliteration is useful in corpus alignment, cross-language information retrieval and extraction. It is also a good supplement to general machine translation systems for handling out-of-vocabulary-words.

In this paper, we present a novel transliteration system that is composed of various types of neural networks. First, we preprocess the training data, pairs of parallel person names, to retrieve segmentations of the transliteration units and their alignments in an unsupervised fashion by using the M2M aligner (Jiampojamarn et al., 2007). We start to build the neural network from the character level afterwards. A convolutional layer is employed to capture the information encoded in the character sequences. With respect to the transliteration units, the outputs of convolutional layers are

fed into a recurrent neural network for sequence to sequence transaction.

Our systems are trained and evaluated on the official English to Chinese and Chinese to English datasets provided by the NEWS 2016 transliteration shared task (Zhang et al., 2016). We also compare our neural network model with the best performing phrase-based system on English-Chinese transliteration in the 2015 shared task (Shao et al., 2015) that is built with the popular machine translation framework Moses (Koehn et al., 2007).

2 Background

The classical joint source-channel model (Li et al., 2004) is one of the early successful approaches for machine transliteration, which is a generative Hidden Markov Model (HMM) that directly maps the source names into target names via passing them through a trained source channel. Later, Conditional Random Fields (CRF) (Lafferty et al., 2001) as a more powerful discriminative model for sequence labelling is adapted for transliteration and yields very competitive results. For the sake of efficiency, the CRF based systems are mostly pipeline models that process segmentation and mapping separately (Kuo et al., 2012).

A substantial number of state-of-the-art systems are phrase-based transliteration models that view transliteration as character-level translation without distortion. The phrase-based system is reasonably efficient. More importantly, it is capable of resolving some segmentation errors and therefore acquires better overall performance.

In recent years, neural network models obtain remarkable success in a wide range of natural language processing tasks. Collobert et al. (2011) apply generic neural network architectures to several sequence labelling tasks and obtain competitive results despite of the task-specific variations. De-

Proceedings of the Sixth Named Entity Workshop, joint with 54th ACL, pages 73–77,
Berlin, Germany, August 12, 2016. ©2016 Association for Computational Linguistics

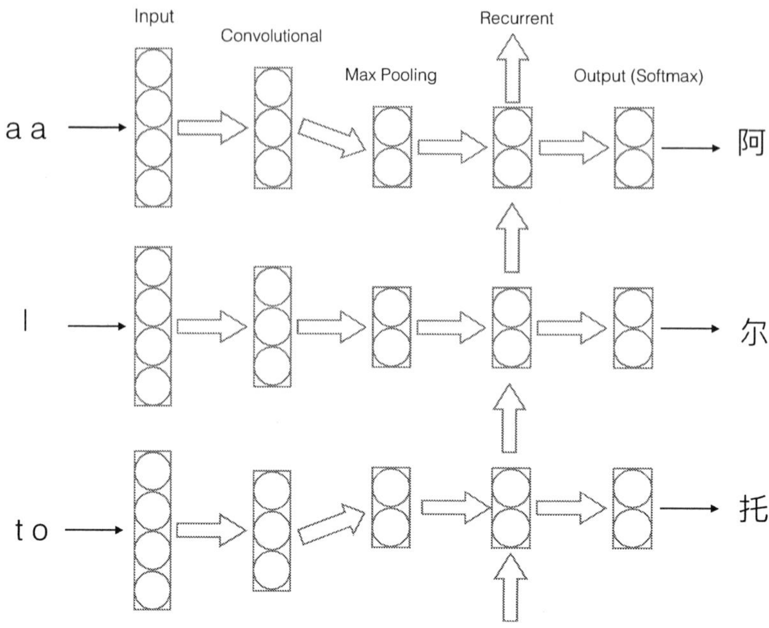

Figure 1: Architecture of the Neural Network

selaers et al. (2009) use deep belief networks for Arabic-English transliteration. Finch et al. (2015) augment the traditional phrase-based system with generation probabilities from neural networks as additional features.

3 System Description

3.1 Retrieving Transliteration Units

For English-Chinese transliteration, multiple English letters are usually mapped into one single Chinese character. In our system, we regard those concatenated substrings and individual Chinese characters as fundamental transliteration units for constructing the transliteration systems. We adopt the M2M aligner that uses an Expectation-Maximisation (EM) algorithm to obtain the alignments as well as boundaries of transliteration units on the English side. We aim to retrieve high quality alignments of the M2M aligner by following the settings described in Shao et al. (2015). We also adopt the same pre-processing and post-processing techniques, which includes pre-contracting some letters, manipulating the boundaries of those alignments associated with the letter 'x' and using an EM algorithm to reduce the errors by eliminating low frequent segmentations and alignments.

3.2 Building the Neural Networks

Figure 1 shows the architecture of the neural network that we designed for the transliteration task.

For the transliteration from English to Chinese, the segmented substrings as the basic transliteration units are directly fed into the input layer as strings of separated letters. Those letters are simply initialised as one-hot vectors. In order to apply the convolutional layer over the transliteration units, all the substrings are padded with a special letter <PADDING> to make them have the same length as the longest one.

For Chinese to English, we use a Character-Pinyin dictionary to convert the Chinese characters into their romanisations. The romanised characters can be used by the input layer similarly as strings of letters. The same padding approach is used. In addition, we preserve the tones and add them as extra information to the neural network. The tones are represented similarly as one-hot vectors and concatenated with the character vectors that represent the Pinyin of the corresponding Chinese characters.

We assume that the information required by transliteration is encoded in the strings composed by letters on the source side. Moreover, those letters contribute differently to transliteration. Some letters in English names are not pronounced and therefore can be regarded as noise. After the input layer, we add a one-dimensional convolutional layer followed by a regular max-pooling layer, which is expected to filter out the noise as well as capture which letters are more crucial to transliteration.

Since transliteration is a sequence to sequence transcription, we stack a recurrent layer on top of the convolutional layer to handle the dependencies between the transliteration units. Considering the fact that transliteration is a completely linear procedure without any hierarchical structures involved, our model employs the simple recurrent neural network (SimpleRNN) instead of the more prevalent Long-Short-Term-Memory (LSTM) (Hochreiter and Schmidhuber, 1997). Our experiments also indicate that there is no significant difference between the two in accuracy while training SimpleRNN is much faster.

The output layer is a time-distributed dense layer that uses softmax as the activation function to map the outputs of recurrent layer into the target representations. We simply adopt the tags which yield the highest probabilities in the output probability distributions of the neural networks.

3.3 Configurations and Hyper-parameters

We use Keras (Chollet, 2015), a deep learning Python package that uses Theano as backend to implement our neural network.

Considering that the one-hot vector representations are very sparse, we use 200 convolutional kernels with 2 as the filter length. The pooling length of the max-pooling layer is 2 without stride. We use Rectified Linear Unit (relu) as the activation function.

The chosen output size of the recurrent layer is 200. The stateful option is enabled so that the states for the samples of each batch will be reused as initial states for the samples in the next batch. The employed activation function is Hyperbolic Tangent (tanh).

There are two dropout layers (Srivastava et al., 2014) added respectively after the max-pooling layer and recurrent layer with the same drop rate 0.2 to mitigate overfitting.

The batch size used for English to Chinese and Chinese to English are respectively 30 and 100 for the reason that there are many more target tags in Chinese to English transliteration. Assigning a bigger batch size for the transliteration model of Chinese to English saves a significant amount of training time.

The objective function used for our model is Categorical Cross-Entropy along with RMSprop as the optimiser.

3.4 Training

Following the requirements of the standard run, we use the official training data to train our neural network with error back-propagation. The development sets are used as the validation data. We inspect the accuracy in terms of the official evaluation metrics ACC and F-score (Zhang et al., 2016) after each epoch.

For English to Chinese, after approximately 50 epochs, the model converges and the accuracy scores randomly swing in a certain range. It requires about 70 epochs for Chinese to English.

In our experiments, we use fixed numbers of epochs, 150 for English to Chinese and 200 for Chinese to English. The experiments are performed on a normal Intel Core i7 CPU. For English to Chinese, each epoch takes around 125 seconds and for Chinese to English it is around 170 seconds. Training the Chinese to English transliteration model also requires a comparatively larger memory (at least 4 GB). We use the models of the top ten best epochs to decode the test data for final submission.

3.5 Decoding

For English to Chinese, the boundaries of transliteration units are required at the decoding stage. The English source names in the test set need to be segmented before being passed to the neural network. In this paper, we train a trivial LSTM as our segmentation system. The segmentation is modelled as a tagging procedure. We use binary tags to indicate whether a letter is the end of a transliteration unit. An extra tag indicating whether the letter is a vowel or consonant is fed as additional information. The output size of the recurrent layer is 50. The batch size is 35 and it is trained for 40 epochs. The system is trained with the English part of the English to Chinese training data that are segmented by the M2M aligner. We slice 10% of the data for validation.

For Chinese to English, the test dataset is preprocessed with the Character-Pinyin dictionary in the same way as the training data.

Task	System	ACC	F-score	MRR	MAP
English to Chinese	Phrase-based SMT	0.335	0.676	0.396	0.323
	Neural Network	0.281	0.643	0.301	0.281
	Baseline	0.194	0.585	0.194	0.183
Chinese to English	Phrase-based SMT	0.199	0.752	0.281	0.195
	Neural Network	0.162	0.725	0.182	0.162
	Baseline	0.098	0.646	0.098	0.095

Table 1: Official Results

4 Experimental Results

Table 1 shows the experimental results of our neural network model. In addition, we include two other systems for comparison. The baseline system is a naive character-level system built with Moses. The scores of the baseline are provided by the shared task organiser. The Phrase-based SMT is the back-off model introduced in Shao et al. (2015), which is a state-of-the-art phrase-based system as well as the best performing system on English-Chinese transliteration in the previous year's shared task.

Our neural network system outperforms the baseline by a large margin and it is competitive compared to the other evaluated transliteration systems in this year's shared task, which indicates that employing convolutional neural networks in conjunction with a simple recurrent neural network is a feasible approach for transliteration.

The ACC and MRR scores of the neural network models in both transliteration directions are not significantly different, which reveals that there are no significant distinctions between the models of the ten best epochs according to their outputs.

The Phrase-based SMT system remains very successful and outperforms the neural network model significantly. The primary reason is that the phrase-based model has a very powerful higher-order language model to harmonise the generated transliteration as a whole sequence. It is also capable of resolving some segmentation errors via utilising more coarse-grained phrases as transliteration units, whereas the neural network heavily depends on the quality of segmentation.

Besides, for English to Chinese, the neural network model is actually a pipeline system that handles segmentation and decoding separately similarly to the CRF-based models. The errors arising at the segmentation stage will propagate to the decoding stage and inevitably detriment the overall transliteration accuracy. For Chinese to English, we use the romanisations of the Chinese characters to build the transliteration system. It is quite possible that some useful information in the characters for transliteration is lost during the conversion.

5 Future Work

We will continue exploring and delving into different neural network models for transliteration, including experimenting with different architectures and doing more hyper-parameter tuning.

For English to Chinese transliteration, we will aim to build a joint model to substitute the pipeline model, which will make the neural network model less dependent on the segmentation quality. For Chinese to English, ideally the Chinese characters instead of their romanisations will be used as the basic units to construct the transliteration system. The properties of the characters, such as numbers of strokes, different types of radicals are expected to be effectively used by the convolutional neural networks.

6 Conclusions

We successfully apply neural network models on English-Chinese machine transliteration tasks in this work. We use convolutional layers to extract information from the character sequences of basic transliteration units. The output is passed to a simple recurrent layer afterwards for sequence to sequence transcription. The official evaluation results demonstrate that our neural network model is competitive while there is still a notable gap to the best performing phrase-based transliteration system.

References

Franois Chollet. 2015. Keras. `https://github.com/fchollet/keras`.

Ronan Collobert, Jason Weston, Léon Bottou, Michael Karlen, Koray Kavukcuoglu, and Pavel Kuksa. 2011. Natural language processing (almost) from scratch. *J. Mach. Learn. Res.*, 12:2493–2537, November.

Thomas Deselaers, Saša Hasan, Oliver Bender, and Hermann Ney. 2009. A deep learning approach to machine transliteration. In *Proceedings of the Fourth Workshop on Statistical Machine Translation*, pages 233–241. Association for Computational Linguistics.

Andrew Finch, Lemao Liu, Xiaolin Wang, and Eiichiro Sumita. 2015. Neural network transduction models in transliteration generation. In *Proceedings of NEWS 2015 The Fifth Named Entities Workshop*, page 61.

Sepp Hochreiter and Jürgen Schmidhuber. 1997. Long short-term memory. *Neural computation*, 9(8):1735–1780.

Sittichai Jiampojamarn, Grzegorz Kondrak, and Tarek Sherif. 2007. Applying many-to-many alignments and hidden markov models to letter-to-phoneme conversion. In *Human Language Technologies 2007: The Conference of the North American Chapter of the Association for Computational Linguistics; Proceedings of the Main Conference*, pages 372–379, Rochester, New York, April. Association for Computational Linguistics.

Philipp Koehn, Hieu Hoang, Alexandra Birch, Chris Callison-Burch, Marcello Federico, Nicola Bertoldi, Brooke Cowan, Wade Shen, Christine Moran, Richard Zens, Chris Dyer, Ondřej Bojar, Alexandra Constantin, and Evan Herbst. 2007. Moses: Open source toolkit for statistical machine translation. In *Proceedings of the 45th Annual Meeting of the ACL on Interactive Poster and Demonstration Sessions*, ACL '07, pages 177–180, Stroudsburg, PA, USA. Association for Computational Linguistics.

Chan-Hung Kuo, Shih-Hung Liu, Tian-Jian Mike Jiang, Cheng-Wei Lee, and Wen-Lian Hsu, 2012. *Proceedings of the 4th Named Entity Workshop (NEWS) 2012*, chapter Cost-benefit Analysis of Two-Stage Conditional Random Fields based English-to-Chinese Machine Transliteration, pages 76–80. Association for Computational Linguistics.

John D. Lafferty, Andrew McCallum, and Fernando C. N. Pereira. 2001. Conditional random fields: Probabilistic models for segmenting and labeling sequence data. In *Proceedings of the Eighteenth International Conference on Machine Learning*, ICML '01, pages 282–289, San Francisco, CA, USA. Morgan Kaufmann Publishers Inc.

Haizhou Li, Min Zhang, and Jian Su. 2004. A joint source-channel model for machine transliteration. In *Proceedings of the 42Nd Annual Meeting on Association for Computational Linguistics*, ACL '04, Stroudsburg, PA, USA. Association for Computational Linguistics.

Yan Shao, Jörg Tiedemann, and Joakim Nivre. 2015. Boosting english-chinese machine transliteration via high quality alignment and multilingual resources. In *Proceedings of NEWS 2015 The Fifth Named Entities Workshop*, page 56.

Nitish Srivastava, Geoffrey Hinton, Alex Krizhevsky, Ilya Sutskever, and Ruslan Salakhutdinov. 2014. Dropout: A simple way to prevent neural networks from overfitting. *The Journal of Machine Learning Research*, 15(1):1929–1958.

Min Zhang, Haizhou Li, A. Kumaranz, and Rafael E. Banchs. 2016. Whitepaper of NEWS 2016 shared task on transliteration generation. In *NEWS '16 Proceedings of the 2016 Named Entities Workshop: Shared Task on Transliteration*, Berlin, Germany.

Target-Bidirectional Neural Models for Machine Transliteration

Andrew Finch and **Lemao Liu** and **Xiaolin Wang** and **Eiichiro Sumita**
National Institute of Information and Communications Technology (NICT)
Advanced Translation Technology Laboratory
3-5 Hikaridai
Keihanna Science City
619-0289 JAPAN
{andrew.finch,lmliu,xiaolin.wang,eiichiro.sumita}@nict.go.jp

Abstract

Our purely neural network-based system represents a paradigm shift away from the techniques based on phrase-based statistical machine translation we have used in the past. The approach exploits the agreement between a pair of target-bidirectional LSTMs, in order to generate balanced targets with both good suffixes and good prefixes. The evaluation results show that the method is able to match and even surpass the current state-of-the-art on most language pairs, but also exposes weaknesses on some tasks motivating further study. The Janus toolkit that was used to build the systems used in the evaluation is publicly available at https://github.com/lemaoliu/Agtarbidir.

1 Introduction

Our primary system for the NEWS shared evaluation on transliteration generation is different in character from all our previous systems. In past years, all our systems have been based on phrase-based statistical machine translation (PB-SMT) techniques, stemming from the system proposed in (Finch and Sumita, 2008). This year's system is a pure end-to-end neural network transducer. In (Finch et al., 2012) auxiliary neural network language models (both monolingual and bilingual (Li et al., 2004)) were introduced as features to augment the log-linear model of a phrase-based transduction system, and led to modest gains in system performance. In the NEWS 2015 workshop (Finch et al., 2015) neural transliteration systems using attention-based sequence-to-sequence neural network transducers (Bahdanau et al., 2014) were applied to transliteration generation. In isolation, the performance was found to be lower than that of the phrase-based system on all of the

tasks, however we observed that the neural network transducer was very effective when used as a model for re-scoring the output of the phrase-based transduction process, and this led to respectable improvements relative to previous systems on most of the tasks.

Our focus this year has been on the development of an end-to-end purely neural network-based system capable of competitive performance. The changes and improvements over the sequence-to-sequence neural transducer used in NEWS2015 are as follows:

- A target-bidirectional agreement model was employed.

- Ensembles of neural networks were used rather than just a single network.

- The ensembles were selected from different training runs and different training epochs according to their performance on development (and test) data.

In all our experiments we have taken a strictly language independent approach. Each of the language pairs was processed automatically from the character sequence representation supplied for the shared tasks, with no language specific treatment for any of the language pairs. Furthermore no preprocessing was performed on any of the data with the exception of uppercasing the English to ensure consistency among the data sets.

2 System Description

2.1 Target-bidirectional Models

Our system uses the target-bidirectional approach proposed in (Liu et al., 2016), and the reader is referred to this paper for a full description of the method we employ. In brief, we use pairs of LSTM RNN sequence-to-sequence transducers that first

Proceedings of the Sixth Named Entity Workshop, joint with 54th ACL, pages 78–82,
Berlin, Germany, August 12, 2016. ©2016 Association for Computational Linguistics

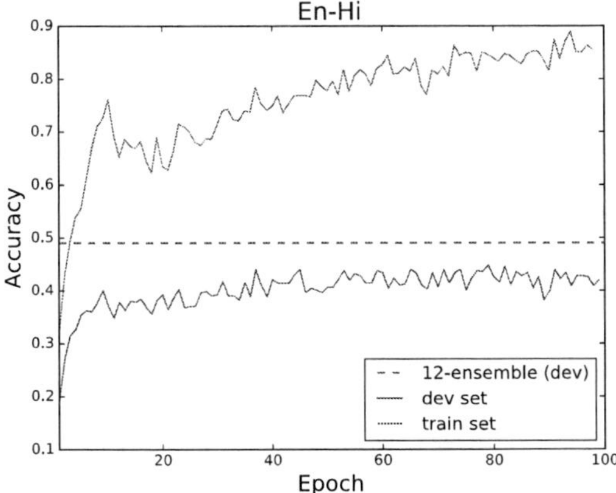

Figure 1: En-Hi training performance.

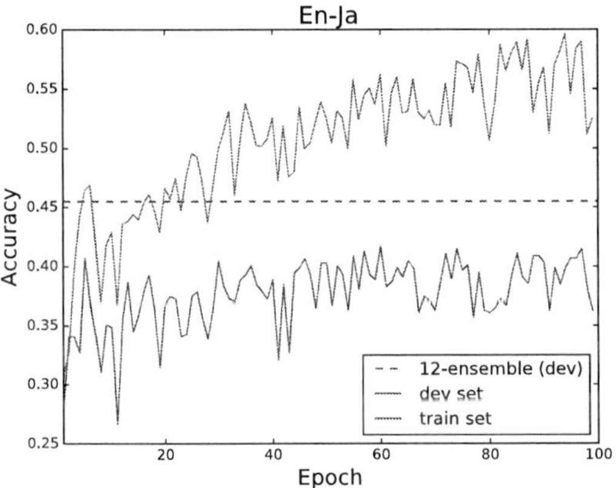

Figure 2: En-Ja training performance.

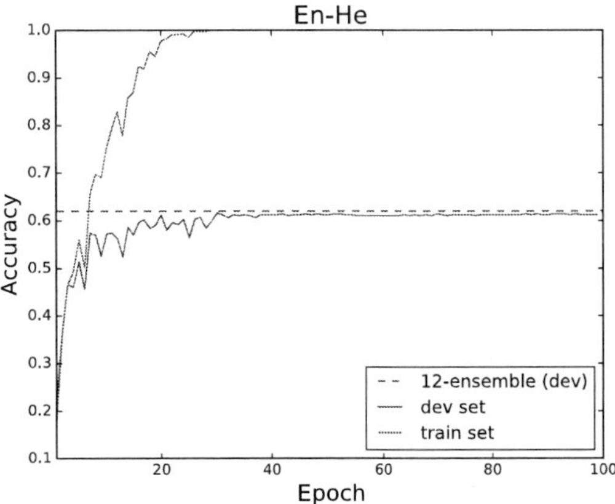

Figure 3: En-He training performance.

encode the input sequence into a fixed length vector, and then *decode* from this to produce the target. The method mitigates a fundamental shortcoming in neural sequence-to-sequence transduction, in which errors in prediction accumulate in the context vectors used to make the predictions, leading to progressively worse performance as the generation process proceeds. The result is unbalanced output which has high quality prefixes that degrade to lower quality suffixes. Our bidirectional agreement model overcomes this by using a pair of RNNs that generate from both left-to-right and right-to-left, producing 2 k-bests lists which are combined[1] in order to encourage agreement between the models. In (Liu et al., 2016) it is shown that the resulting output is both more balanced and of substantially higher quality than that resulting from either unidirectional model. Furthermore it

is shown that the gains from this method cannot be obtained from larger ensembles of unidirectional models. The approach was shown to be effective in both grapheme-to-phoneme conversion (where it set a new state-of-the-art benchmark), and in English-Japanese transliteration. This paper evaluates the method on a much wider variety of tasks highlighting some of the strengths and weaknesses of the new approach.

2.2 Ensembles

Multiple neural networks were combined into ensembles. This was done by linear interpolation (with equal weights) of the probability distributions produced by the networks over the target vocabulary during the beam search decoding.

3 Experimental Methodology

3.1 Corpora

The neural networks were trained on all of the data for each task, with the exception of 500 pairs which were used for development. The development data was used in order to determine whether or not the networks had fully trained, and also as a means of selecting the neural network models that comprised the ensembles.

In this year's workshop, 15 runs on the test data were permitted. 12 of the runs were used to evaluate the models to be used in the ensembles, and the remaining 3 runs were used to determine the ensemble size. In order to remove the advantage of using test data during system development (to maintain cross-comparability with previous years' results), one of the ensembles used was composed of all 12 of the networks ('12-ensemble' in Figure 1).

---

[1] In all experiments reported here we used the joint *k*-best approximation method.

In addition, in order to observe the performance of the models on the training set during training, a sample of 1000 pairs was taken from the training data.

3.2 Training

Each of the systems was trained for 100 epochs. For all language pairs the accuracy on the development set appeared to stop improving after approximately 50 epochs. Graphs showing the performance of the systems during training are shown in Figure 1 which represent typical training runs, together with interesting exceptions in Figures 3 and 2. The green (upper) solid line on the graphs represents the accuracy on training data, the blue (lower) solid line represents the accuracy on unseen development data, and the dashed purple line represents the performance of an ensemble composed of the best performing 12 neural networks on the development set.

The curves in Figure 1 are typical, with the performance of the system on training data still steadily increasing at epoch 100, but with the performance on development data reaching its maximum value often by epoch 20, and almost always by epoch 50. We therefore conclude that the networks are all fully trained after 50 epochs. Furthermore, we did not observe any noticable degradation in performance after epoch 50 due to overfitting.

The curves in Figures 2 and 3 are atypical. On En-Ja the variance in accuracy from epoch to epoch was unusually high. The gains from using ensembles of networks were also larger than for other language pairs. In addition, the accuracy on training data remained lower than most language pairs. The curves for En-He show the opposite behavior. The accuracy on training data is 1.0 after about 35 epochs indicating that the neural network has effectively memorized the training data. At this point the variance in accuracy from epoch to epoch falls to almost zero. The gains from using ensembles for this language pair are very small.

We were unable to train a neural network with high accuracy on the Ar-En dataset, and as a consequence did not enter a system on this task this year. The reasons for this are not yet clear, but the system had reasonably good f-scores with very low accuracy. The networks seemed able to produce plausible output, that was rarely an exact match with the reference. We believe the neural network may have been able to generalize from the data, but was not able to memorize it well.

Training times were dependent on the language pair. Most language pairs completed the 100-epoch training on a single Tesla K40m GPU in under a day. Training for the Arabic-English task was around 10 times longer due to the larger training set.

3.3 Ensemble Selection

In order to form ensembles we need to select the ensemble size, and also the neural networks that will comprise the ensemble. In pilot experiments, we found that it is possible to obtain respectable improvement by building ensembles from the networks at different epochs during training. Our strategy was to train 5 target-bidirectional RNNs for each language pair, and select the ensemble from the epochs within these 5 runs.

In this year's workshop, 15 evaluations were permitted on test data for each task. We used 12 of these to evaluate the target-bidirectional RNNs, and 3 to select the ensemble size from $\{4, 8, 12\}$. The ensembles of size 12 were selected using development data only as follows: the best 2 target-bidirectional RNNs were selected from epochs of each of the 5 training runs, then the best 2 target-bidirectional RNNs were chosen from the remaining epochs/runs. Ensembles of 4 and 8 were selected from the candidate set of 12 (that were selected using the development set), according to their accuracy on the test data. We found a moderate positive correlation between training and development set accuracy at each epoch of the training. This suggests that the variance in the accuracy of networks from epoch to epoch during training is not simply random noise, but that 'good' and 'bad' networks exist at different epochs, and this motivated our strategy to select them based on development set accuracy.

3.4 Architecture and Parameters

The network architecture for all of the networks used in all tasks was the same, and was chosen because it has proven to be effective in other experiments. The computational expense associated with working with neural networks on this task prohibited us from running experiments to select the optimal architecture, and therefore it is possible that architectures that are considerably better than the one we have chosen exist.

The RNNs consisted of a single layer of 500 LSTMs, with 500-unit embeddings on the source and target sides. AdaDelta (Zeiler, 2012) was used for training with a minibatch size of 16. A beam

Language Pair		2012 system	2015 system	2016 Baseline	2016 12-ensemble	2016 Primary
English to Bengali	(EnBa)	0.460	0.483	0.287	**0.498**	**0.498**
Chinese to English	(ChEn)	0.203	0.184	0.098	0.211	**0.214**
English to Chinese	(EnCh)	0.311	0.313	0.193	0.309	**0.316**
English to Hebrew	(EnHe)	0.154	0.179	0.109	0.184	**0.189**
English to Hindi	(EnHi)	0.668	0.696	0.270	0.709	**0.715**
English to Japanese Katakana	(EnJa)	0.401	0.407	0.209	0.464	**0.465**
English to Kannada	(EnKa)	0.546	0.562	0.196	0.570	**0.583**
English to Korean Hangul	(EnKo)	**0.384**	0.363	0.218	0.348	0.352
English to Persian	(EnPe)	0.655	**0.697**	0.482	0.691	0.696
English to Tamil	(EnTa)	0.592	0.626	0.258	0.613	**0.629**
English to Thai	(EnTh)	0.122	0.157	0.068	0.179	**0.187**
English to Japanese Kanji	(JnJk)	0.513	**0.610**	0.461	0.327	0.327
Thai to English	(ThEn)	0.140	0.154	0.091	0.194	**0.196**

Table 1: The official evaluation results in terms of the top-1 accuracy.

search with beam width 12 was used to obtain the k-best hypotheses. Decoding was aborted, and a null hypothesis output when a target sequence was generated that was three times longer than the source (sequences of length less than 6 were not aborted).

4 Evaluation Results

The official scores for our system are given in Table 1, alongside the scores of our previous systems on the same test set, and the scores of the official baseline system. The highest scores are highlighted in bold, and it is clear that this year's system has attained higher accuracy than the systems from previous years on most of the language pairs. For some pairs, such as English-Katakana, English-Thai and Thai-English, the improvement is substantial. However, there are also tasks in which the neural system was not able to match the performance of the previous system, notably English-Japanese Kanji, English-Hangul and Arabic-English. The first two of these tasks have quite large vocabularies on the target side, and this may make them less suitable for a neural approach. The Arabic-English task has no such issues, and furthermore has a far larger training corpus available which ought to favor the neural method, however it differs from the other tasks in that short vowels are not represented in written Arabic, but must still be generated on the target side. Further research is necessary to determine the true cause, but our conjecture is that phrase-based systems, which effectively memorize the training data in a piecewise manner, are consequently more suc-

cessful on this task than neural networks which are geared more towards generalization rather than memorization.

5 Conclusion

The system used for this year's shared evaluation signals a paradigm shift away from the phrase-based systems based on machine translation technology used by our group in earlier years. Our end-to-end neural machine transliteration system leverages the agreement between target-bidirectional RNN ensembles to improve its performance. On most of the transliteration tasks the system has shown itself to be capable of matching and even surpassing the current state-of-the-art. We believe neural networks have a bright future in the field of transliteration generation, and the experiments on the NEWS Workshop datasets have uncovered outstanding issues that will make interesting topics for future research as this technology matures.

Acknowledgements

For the English-Japanese, English-Korean and Arabic-English datasets, the reader is referred to the CJK website: http://www.cjk.org. For English-Hindi, English-Tamil, and English-Kannada, and English-Bangla the data sets originated from the work of (Kumaran and Kellner, 2007) [2]. The Chinese language corpora came from the Xinhua news agency (Xinhua News Agency, 1992). The English Persian corpus originates from the work of (Karimi et al., 2006; Karimi et al., 2007).

[2] http://research.microsoft.com/india

References

Dzmitry Bahdanau, Kyunghyun Cho, and Yoshua Bengio. 2014. Neural machine translation by jointly learning to align and translate. *CoRR*.

Andrew Finch and Eiichiro Sumita. 2008. Phrase-based machine transliteration. In *Proceedings of the 3rd International Joint Conference on Natural Language Processing (IJCNLP)*, volume 1, Hyderabad, India.

Andrew Finch, Paul Dixon, and Eiichiro Sumita. 2012. Rescoring a phrase-based machine transliteration system with recurrent neural network language models. In *Proceedings of the 4th Named Entity Workshop (NEWS) 2012*, pages 47–51, Jeju, Korea, July. Association for Computational Linguistics.

Andrew Finch, Lemao Liu, Xiaolin Wang, and Eiichiro Sumita. 2015. Neural network transduction models in transliteration generation. In *Proceedings of the Fifth Named Entity Workshop*, pages 61–66, Beijing, China, July. Association for Computational Linguistics.

Sarvnaz Karimi, Andrew Turpin, and Falk Scholer. 2006. English to persian transliteration. In *SPIRE*, pages 255–266.

Sarvnaz Karimi, Andrew Turpin, and Falk Scholer. 2007. Corpus effects on the evaluation of automated transliteration systems. *Proceedings of the 45th Annual Meeting of the Association of Computational Linguistics*.

A. Kumaran and Tobias Kellner. 2007. A generic framework for machine transliteration. In *SIGIR '07*, pages 721–722.

Haizhou Li, Min Zhang, and Jian Su. 2004. A joint source-channel model for machine transliteration. In *ACL '04: Proceedings of the 42nd Annual Meeting on Association for Computational Linguistics*, page 159, Morristown, NJ, USA. Association for Computational Linguistics.

Lemao Liu, Andrew Finch, Masao Utiyama, and Eiichiro Sumita. 2016. Agreement on target-bidirectional lstms for sequence-to-sequence learning. In *Thirtieth AAAI Conference on Artificial Intelligence*.

Xinhua News Agency. 1992. Chinese transliteration of foreign personal names. *The Commercial Press*.

Matthew D. Zeiler. 2012. ADADELTA: an adaptive learning rate method. *CoRR*, abs/1212.5701.

Regulating Orthography-Phonology Relationship
for English to Thai Transliteration

Binh Minh Nguyen
National University of
Singapore, Singapore
nguyen.binh.minh92@u.nus.edu

Gia H. Ngo
National University of
Singapore, Singapore
ngohgia@u.nus.edu

Nancy F. Chen
Institute for Infocomm
Research, Singapore
nfychen@i2r.a-star.edu.sg

Abstract

In this paper, we discuss our endeavors
for the Named Entities Workshop (NEWS)
2016 transliteration shared task, where we
focus on English to Thai transliteration.
The alignment between Thai orthography
and phonology is not always monotonous,
but few transliteration systems take this
into account. In our proposed system,
we exploit phonological knowledge to
resolve problematic instances where the
monotonous alignment assumption breaks
down. We achieve a 29% relative improvement over the baseline system for the
NEWS 2016 transliteration shared task.

1 Introduction

Transliteration is the process of transform-
ing a word from one writing system (source
word) to a word in another writing system (target
word) (Knight and Graehl, 1998). Transliteration
is often used to borrow names and technical terms
from the source language into the target language
when translation is difficult or awkward. For example, *British* is transliterated into Thai as [*bri-tit*
] using Royal Thai General System of Transcription (RTGS) notation (Royal Institute, 1999).

Transliteration can be formulated as a special
case of translation. Instead of converting words
from one language to the semantically equivalent
words in another language, transliteration converts
the source word to a phonetically equivalent target
word (Knight and Graehl, 1998).

In transliteration, character-reordering is important to ensure the transliterated words follow the phonotactic rules of the target language.
Character-reordering in transliteration is similar to
word-reordering in translation, where the trans-
lated sentence needs to satisfy the grammatical
rules of the target language. However, most

transliteration systems do not take into account
character-reordering.

If the phonetically equivalent characters are
reordered in the target word, the source word
and the transliterated word are said to be non-
monotonously aligned (Toms and Casacuberta,
2006). A classical approach to transliteration is
using phrase-based Statistical Machine Translation (pbSMT). While pbSMT approach can model
non-monotonous alignment of characters in the
transliteration task, the pbSMT systems introduced in Kunchukuttan and Bhattacharyya (2015),
Nicolai et al. (2015) and Finch et al. (2015) did not
model such character-reordering. In addition to
pbSMT, Nicolai et al. (2015) also used grapheme-
to-phoneme (G2P) conversion tools, namely Di-
recTL+ (Jiampojamarn et al., 2010) and Sequitur
G2P (Bisani and Ney, 2008), for the transliteration task. Such G2P conversion tools also make a
similar assumption of monotonous alignment between source and target word. While this assumption is reasonable for transliteration between most
language pairs, there are cases in English to Thai
transliteration whereby this assumption is invalid.

In this paper, we regulate the relationship between Thai orthography and phonology in the English to Thai transliteration task. We show that the
transliteration accuracy can be improved by addressing the mismatch between Thai orthography
and phonology that causes the monotonous alignment assumption to break down.

2 Thai Phonology

2.1 Syllable

A syllable is considered the basic unit of a word
in both written and spoken language (Ladefoged
and Johnson, 2014). Most languages have the
following syllable structure, including English
and Thai (Kessler and Treiman, 1997; Luksaneeyanawin, 1992):

83

Proceedings of the Sixth Named Entity Workshop, joint with 54th ACL, pages 83–87,
Berlin, Germany, August 12, 2016. ©2016 Association for Computational Linguistics

$$[O] \quad N \quad [Cd] \quad [T] \qquad (1)$$

where O, N, Cd, T denotes onset, nucleus, coda, tone respectively.

In Thai, an onset (O) has at most two consonants and a coda (Cd) has at most one consonant, while a nucleus (N) can be a vowel or a diphthong (Luksaneeyanawin, 1992). Tone (T) is a feature of many tonal languages (Yip, 2002). Tone is a variation in pitch that is used to distinguish different words (Yip, 2002). For example, both the Thai words *value* and *to trade* have the same syllable [*khaa*] (RTGS), but *value* is pronounced with a falling tone while *to trade* is pronounced with a high tone.

The aim of transliteration is to generate a word in the target language that best matches the pronunciation of the word in the source language (Knight and Graehl, 1998). Although the syllable structure in English and in Thai are similar, the idiosyncratic relationship between Thai pronunciation and Thai orthography makes English to Thai transliteration complex.

1. In Thai orthography, the position of the onset and nucleus can be inverted for a syllable with a leading vowel (Chotimongkol and Black, 2000). A leading vowel is part of the syllable's nucleus. While the vowels of the nucleus are pronounced after the consonants of the onset as specified by the syllable structure in (1), leading vowels precede the consonants of the onset in written form. The order of consonants and vowels in Thai written form therefore does not always match the pronunciation order. This is unlike English whereby the order of consonants and vowels in the written form matches the order in pronunciation. For example, *Reagan* is transliterated into Thai as [*er-aekn*] (RTGS) but is pronounced in Thai as [reːkɛːn] (IPA). [*e*] and [*ea*] are leading vowels and are written before their corresponding onset which are [*r*] and [*k*] respectively.

2. Lexical tones in Thai are not uniquely defined by tone marks, but are determined by the type of the syllable, the class of the onset consonant, and the length of the nucleus (Smyth, 2002). For example, the Thai words for both *to pass* and *glancing* are pronounced with a low tone. However, only *to pass* has a tone

mark in Thai script, while *glancing* does not.

3. Some vowels are implicit in certain phonetic contexts (Chotimongkol and Black, 2000). Such vowels are present when the syllable is pronounced but it is omitted when the syllable is transcribed. For example, *Steve* is transliterated as [*s-tip*] but is pronounced as [sa-tip] (RTGS). In this case, the vowel [*a*] is implicit.

In this work, we focus on the onset-nucleus inversion case (case 1), which occurs much more often.

2.2 Alignment between Thai Orthography and Phonology

Even though the syllable structure of English and Thai are similar, the mismatch between Thai orthography and Thai syllable structure can lead to challenges in aligning English-Thai transliteration word pairs. In this section, we describe how onset-nucleus inversion may make monotonous alignment difficult.

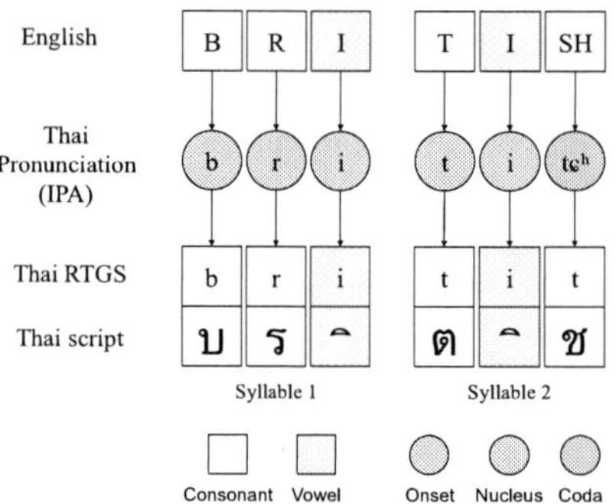

Figure 1: Monotonous Alignment, the source word is *British*

When there is no onset-nucleus inversion such as the case in Figure 1, the alignment between the English word and the Thai word is monotonous.

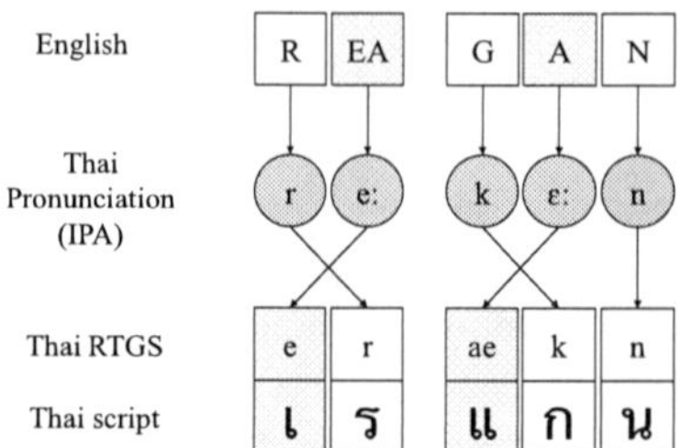

Figure 2: Non-Monotonous alignment of English-Thai transliteration pairs due to onset-nucleus inversion of monophthongs.

However, when onset-nucleus inversion occurs such as the case in Figure 2, the alignment is non-monotonous. Under the monotonous alignment assumption, the English onset [R] may be wrongly aligned to the Thai nucleus [e], and the English nucleus [EA] may be wrongly aligned to the Thai onset [r]. The English syllable [REA] may still be aligned correctly to the Thai syllable [er] if the syllables appear together frequently in the training data. Nevertheless, the presence of onset-nucleus inversion increases the number of possible alignments between English-Thai transliteration pairs.

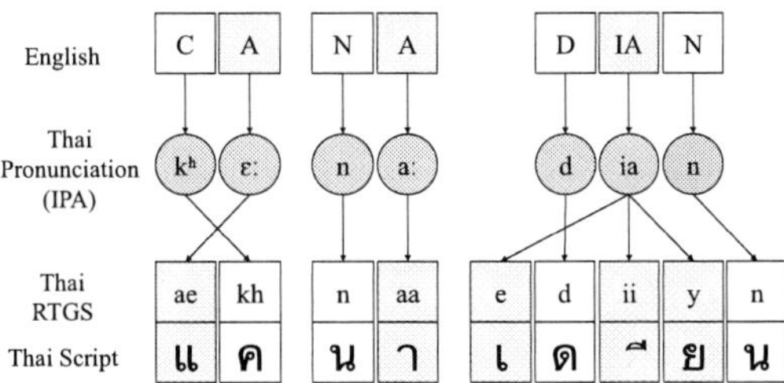

Figure 3: Non-Monotonous alignment of English-Thai transliteration pairs due to onset-nucleus inversion of diphthongs.

Onset-nucleus inversion also occurs in syllables with diphthongs. In Figure 3, the nucleus of the third syllable, namely [e] [ii] [y], is a diphthong in Thai, which comprises of three phonemes [e], [ii] and [y]. Although [e], [ii] and [y] are components of the same nucleus, they are not adjacent. Under the monotonous alignment assumption, it is unclear how to align the English onset, nucleus and coda with Thai onset, nucleus and coda respectively. We attempt to address these issues in the proposed transliteration system.

3 Baseline Systems

We considered two classic approaches as our baseline systems. Transliteration seeks to convert an English string $\mathbf{f} = (f_1, f_2, \ldots, f_n)$ to a Thai string $\mathbf{e} = (e_1, e_2, \ldots, e_m)$.

3.1 Phrase-based Statistical Machine Translation System

Under the pbSMT system, the objective function is given by:

$$\mathbf{e}^* = \arg\max_{\mathbf{e}} p(\mathbf{e})p(\mathbf{f} \mid \mathbf{e}), \qquad (2)$$

where $p(\mathbf{e})$ is estimated from an n-gram language model of Thai, and $p(\mathbf{f} \mid \mathbf{e})$ is estimated from the alignment of segments (phrases) of $\mathbf{f}$ with segments (phrases) of $\mathbf{e}$.

We implement the pbSMT system with the Moses toolkit (Koehn et al., 2007). We use GIZA++ (Och and Ney, 2003) to perform alignment, and SRILM (Stolcke, 2002) to train a 5-gram language model of Thai transliteration units with Witten-Bell smoothing (Witten and Bell, 1991). While the pbSMT systems implemented in (Kunchukuttan and Bhattacharyya, 2015) and (Nicolai et al., 2015) did not model word reordering, we tried various reordering models offered by the Moses toolkit.

3.2 Joint Source-channel System

The baseline system is based on the joint source-channel model, formulated for transliteration in (Li et al., 2004). A similar model (joint sequence model) was proposed for grapheme-to-phoneme conversion in (Bisani and Ney, 2002). We use the Sequitur G2P tool from (Bisani and Ney, 2008) to train the joint source-channel model by assuming a direct correspondence between phoneme and grapheme in the target language.

Given an English string $\mathbf{f}$ and a Thai string $\mathbf{e}$, the joint source-channel model estimates the co-segmentation $\mathbf{q}$, defined as $\mathbf{q} = (q_1, q_2, \ldots, q_n)$ where, $q_i = (f_i, e_i)$, $\mathbf{f} = (f_1, f_2, \ldots, f_n)$ and $\mathbf{e} = (e_1, e_2, \ldots, e_n)$. During decoding, the output Thai string corresponds to the co-segmentation that matches the input English string and yields the maximum likelihood.

The monotonous alignment assumption is built into the joint source-channel model (Bisani and Ney, 2008). Under this assumption, $\forall i < j$, f_i appears before f_j and e_i appears before e_j. In a Thai syllable with onset-nucleus inversion, e_i corresponds to a leading vowel and e_{i+1} corresponds to the onset that comes after the leading vowel. However, f_i and f_{i+1} may still be matched to the onset and nucleus in the English syllable. Therefore, the model may be confused, as the English onset is matched to the Thai nucleus, and the English nucleus is matched to the Thai onset.

4 Proposed Augmented System

The proposed system (Figure 4) augmented the joint source-channel model with a vowel-onset transposition step to regulate the syllable structure.

During training, for Thai syllables with onset-nucleus inversion, the vowel-onset transposition step swaps the location of the leading vowel and the onset consonant (see next page). This swapping ensures that the nucleus always occurs after the onset in a syllable, and vowels that belong to the same nucleus are adjacent in the Thai script.

During decoding, Thai entries that have undergone vowel-onset transposition are reverted back

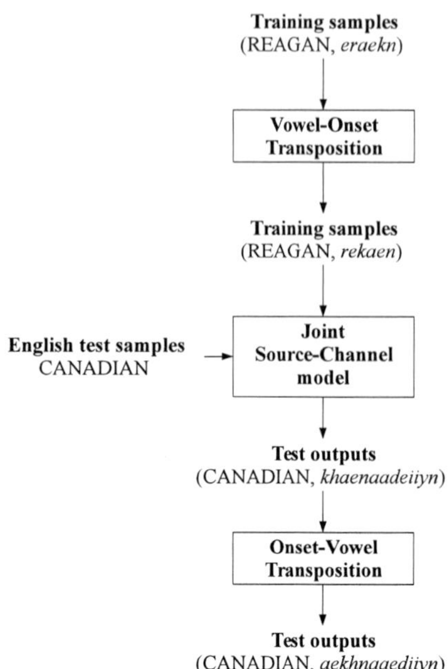

Figure 4: Augmented System. English words are capitalized, Thai words are italicized RTGS.

input : Thai word
output: Regulated Thai word
while *not end of word* **do**
   if *character is leading vowel* **then**
      swap position of vowel and onset;
      go to character after leading vowel;
   else
      go to next character;
   end
end

Vowel-Onset Transposition

via onset-vowel transposition.

5 Experiments

We used the TOP-1 metric (Banchs et al., 2015) for performance comparison between the baseline and the augmented systems. As denoted in Table 1, 75% of the NEWS2016 training set was used for training, the remaining 25% of the NEWS2016 training set was used for tuning, and the NEWS2016 dev set was used for testing. A 6-gram joint source-channel model was used for Baseline joint S-C and Augmented 1. Reordering option *'msd-bidirectional-fe'* in Moses was used for the Baseline pbSMT system as it yielded the best TOP-1 metric.

From Table 2, on the NEWS2016 test set, the

System	Set-up
Baseline pbSMT Baseline joint S-C Augmented 1	Train = 75% NEWS 2016 training Tune = 25% NEWS 2016 training
Augmented 2	Train = NEWS 2016 training Tune = NEWS 2016 dev

Table 1: Data partitioning for the different systems. (pbSMT: phrase-based statistical machine translation, joint S-C: joint source-channel)

System	Dev Set	Test Set
Baseline pbSMT	0.3117	0.111650
Baseline joint S-C	0.3662	0.117314
Augmented 1	0.4015	0.144013
Augmented 2	NA	0.155340

Table 2: Results on NEWS 2016 shared task in terms of TOP-1 accuracy.

augmented system (Augmented 1) achieves a 29% relative improvement over the pbSMT baseline system (Baseline pbSMT), and a 23% relative improvement over the joint source-channel baseline system (Baseline joint S-C).

To observe the performance of the augmented system with the full training data, we trained another separated augmented system (Augmented 2), using both the training set and the dev set data as denoted in Table 1. A 6-gram joint source-channel model was also used for this augmented system. Despite a simpler setup due to exploiting phonology knowledge, this system achieves comparable performance to that of systems reported in (Nicolai et al., 2015) and (Finch et al., 2015) for English to Thai transliteration task.

6 Discussion

Besides the augmented system, we explored a rule-based approach and a phonology-augmented statistical approach for the English to Thai transliteration task. Phonology-augmented statistical approach for English to Vietnamese transliteration has been proposed in (Ngo et al., 2015). These two approaches have inspired the vowel-onset transposition strategy for the joint source-channel model. Despite being similar, our proposed approach takes into account the complex relationship between phonology and orthography, which was not considered in (Ngo et al., 2015). We are working on generalizing this relationship into a statistical model, and also to address other peculiar characteristics of Thai script.

References

Rafael E. Banchs, Min Zhang, Xiangyu Duan, Haizhou Li, and A. Kumaran. 2015. Report of NEWS 2015 Machine Transliteration Shared Task. In *Proceedings of NEWS 2015 The Fifth Named Entities Workshop*, page 10.

Maximilian Bisani and Hermann Ney. 2002. Investigations on joint-multigram models for grapheme-to-phoneme conversion. In *INTERSPEECH*.

Maximilian Bisani and Hermann Ney. 2008. Joint-sequence models for grapheme-to-phoneme conversion. *Speech Communication*, 50(5):434–451.

Ananlada Chotimongkol and Alan W. Black. 2000. Statistically trained orthographic to sound models for Thai. In *INTERSPEECH*, pages 551–554.

Andrew Finch, Lemao Liu, Xiaolin Wang, and Eiichiro Sumita. 2015. Neural Network Transduction Models in Transliteration Generation. In *Proceedings of NEWS 2015 The Fifth Named Entities Workshop*, page 61.

Sittichai Jiampojamarn, Colin Cherry, and Grzegorz Kondrak. 2010. Integrating joint n-gram features into a discriminative training framework.

Brett Kessler and Rebecca Treiman. 1997. Syllable structure and the distribution of phonemes in english syllables. *Journal of Memory and Language*, 37(3):295–311.

Kevin Knight and Jonathan Graehl. 1998. Machine transliteration. *Computational Linguistics*, 24(4):599–612.

Philipp Koehn, Hieu Hoang, Alexandra Birch, Chris Callison-Burch, Marcello Federico, Nicola Bertoldi, Brooke Cowan, Wade Shen, Christine Moran, Richard Zens, et al. 2007. Moses: Open source toolkit for statistical machine translation. In *Proceedings of the 45th annual meeting of the ACL on interactive poster and demonstration sessions*, pages 177–180. Association for Computational Linguistics.

Anoop Kunchukuttan and Pushpak Bhattacharyya. 2015. Data representation methods and use of mined corpora for Indian language transliteration. In *Proceedings of NEWS 2015 The Fifth Named Entities Workshop*, page 78.

Peter Ladefoged and Keith Johnson. 2014. *A course in phonetics*. Cengage learning.

Haizhou Li, Min Zhang, and Jian Su. 2004. A joint source-channel model for machine transliteration. In *Proceedings of the 42nd Annual Meeting on association for Computational Linguistics*, page 159. Association for Computational Linguistics.

Sudaporn Luksaneeyanawin. 1992. Three-dimensional phonology: a historical implication. In *Proceedings of the Third International Symposium on Language and Linguistics: Pan Asiatic Linguistics*, volume 1, pages 75–90.

Hoang Gia Ngo, Nancy F. Chen, Binh Minh Nguyen, Bin Ma, and Haizhou Li. 2015. Phonology-Augmented Statistical Transliteration for Low-Resource Languages. In *Sixteenth Annual Conference of the International Speech Communication Association*.

Garrett Nicolai, Bradley Hauer, Mohammad Salameh, Adam St Arnaud, Ying Xu, Lei Yao, and Grzegorz Kondrak. 2015. Multiple System Combination for Transliteration. In *Proceedings of NEWS 2015 The Fifth Named Entities Workshop*, page 72.

Franz Josef Och and Hermann Ney. 2003. A systematic comparison of various statistical alignment models. *Computational linguistics*, 29(1):19–51.

Royal Institute. 1999. Principles of romanization for thai script by transcription method.

D. Smyth. 2002. *Thai: An Essential Grammar*. Essential grammar. Routledge.

Andreas Stolcke. 2002. Srilm-an extensible language modeling toolkit. In *INTERSPEECH*, volume 2002, page 2002.

Jess Toms and Francisco Casacuberta. 2006. Statistical phrase-based models for interactive computer-assisted translation. In *Proceedings of the COLING/ACL on Main conference poster sessions*, pages 835–841. Association for Computational Linguistics.

Ian H Witten and Timothy C Bell. 1991. The zero-frequency problem: Estimating the probabilities of novel events in adaptive text compression. *Information Theory, IEEE Transactions on*, 37(4):1085–1094.

Moira Yip. 2002. *Tone*. Cambridge University Press.

Moses-based official baseline for NEWS 2016

Marta R. Costa-jussà
TALP Research Center
Universitat Politècnica de Catalunya, Barcelona
`marta.ruiz@upc.edu`

Abstract

Transliteration is the phonetic translation between two different languages. There are many works that approach transliteration using machine translation methods. This paper describes the official baseline system for the NEWS 2016 workshop shared task. This baseline is based on a standard phrase-based machine translation system using Moses. Results are between the range of best and worst from last year's workshops providing a nice starting point for participants this year.

1 Introduction

Transliteration of Name Entities is a useful task for many natural language processing applications such as cross-language information retrieval, information extraction or even machine translation. NEWS workshop has provided for various editions the opportunity to share strategies of transliteration and compare results among different sites. NEWS workshop this year offers training, development and test corpus for 14 language pairs. The final goal of this paper is to offer a baseline system for the NEWS 2016 workshop. Since a general strategy for transliteration has been to use techniques of machine translation, e.g. (Rama and Gali, 2009; David, 2012), we have chosen to use the phrase-based system (Koehn et al., 2003).

The phrase-based machine translation system tries to find the most probable target sentence given the source sentence. The theory behind phrase-based system has evolved from the noisy channel to the log-linear model, which is the one used nowadays. This model combines several feature functions including the translation and language model, the reordering model and the lexical models.

The only requirement to train a phrase-based system is to have a parallel corpus at the level of sentence. In the case of transliteration, we use words as sentences and characters as words. So, for example, parallel sentences to train a transliteration system in English–Hindi is shown in Table 1.

English	Hindi
a a b h a a	अ ा भ ा
a a b h e e r	अ ा भ ी र
a a b i d	अ ा ब ि द
a a b s h a r	अ ा ब श र

Table 1: Example of English-Hindi Parallel Sentences.

Next experimental section describes the preprocessing of the data and the final corpus statistics for the 14 tasks in the evaluation. We report the parameters used to train the phrase-based system. And finally, we explain the results obtained in terms of several automatic measures. After the experimental section, we include a section of conclusions.

2 Experimental framework

This section describes the corpus statistics that we have used, the parameters of the phrase-based system and the results obtained for each one of the 14 tasks: Arabic-to-English (ArEn), Chinese–English (ChEn, EnCh), English—Thai (EnTh, ThEn), English-to-Persian (EnPe), English-to-Hindi (EnHi), English-to-Tamil (EnTa), English-to-Kannada (EnKa), English-to-Bangla (EnBa), English-to-Korean (EnKo), English-to-Hebrew (EnHe), English-to-Japanese (katakana) (EnJa), and English to Japanese (Kanji) (EnJk).

Proceedings of the Sixth Named Entity Workshop, joint with 54th ACL, pages 88–90,
Berlin, Germany, August 12, 2016. ©2016 Association for Computational Linguistics

Languages		Training			Development			Test		
		S	W	V	S	W	V	S	W	V
ArEn	Ar	261.4K	1.5M	38	24,8K	137.9K	38	1.2K	4.5K	6
	En		1.8M	29		181.0K	28		-	-
EnCh/ChEn	Ch	37.7K	119.6K	374	2.7K	9.5K	458	1,0K	2.7K	371
	En		257.7K	26		20K	29	1.0K	6.2K	26
EnTh/ThEn	En	29.6K	210.3K	45	2.0K	14.3K	34	1.2K	8.9K	26
	Th		233.5K	66		15.9K	47	1.2K	10.2K	38
EnPe	En	13.6K	88.0K	26	2.6K	17.0K	26	1.0K	6.3K	26
	Pe		72.3K	43		13.9K	36		-	-
EnHi	En	12.1K	121.7K	44	997	7.1K	26	1,0K	6.3K	27
	Hi		110.9K	83		6.4K	62		-	-
EnTa	En	10.2K	101.9K	42	1.0K	7.2K	29	1.0K	6.3K	27
	Ta		109.7K	63		7.6K	46		-	-
EnKa	En	10.1K	101.0K	42	1.0K	7.2K	30	1.0K	6.3K	27
	Ka		102.6K	75		6.9K	60		-	-
EnBa	En	12.9K	92.7K	30	986	7.0K	27	1,0K	7.0K	27
	Ba		87.8K	62		6.7K	56		-	-
EnKo	En	6.8K	45.4K	28	1.1K	6.1K	26	1.0K	7.5K	28
	Ko		21.4K	714		2.8K	316		-	-
EnHe	En	9.5K	61.3K	32	1.0K	6.4K	26	1,1K	8.1K	28
	He		54.8K	34		5.7K	29		-	-
EnJa	En	31.6K	213.0K	28	1.9K	11.9K	27	1,0K	7,0K	27
	Ja		147.9K	81		8.2K	78		-	-
EnJk	En	23.7K	154.8K	26	3.2K	21.6K	23	1.1K	7.6K	23
	Jk		49,7K	1.6K		6.7K	918		-	-

Table 2: Corpus statistics for training, development and tests sets. S stands for sentences, W for words, and V for vocabulary.

2.1 Data

Table 2 details the corpus statistics for all 14 tasks including training, development and test sets. Pre-processing has been limited to separate characters by a blank space.

2.2 System Description

The phrase-based system was built using Moses (Koehn et al., 2007), version 15th April 2016 from github, with standard parameters, including: grow-final-diag for alignment; Good-Turing smoothing of the relative frequencies; 3-gram language modeling using Kneser-Ney discounting and training with SRILM (Stolcke, 2002); and lexicalized reordering, which includes 6 feature functions. Optimization was done using the MERT algorithm and MBR option for decoding. It is important to note that the same system was used for the 14 tasks without any change or modification.

2.3 Results

Official results are reported in Table 3. In most tasks, results were in the middle of the ranking. Best ranking results were obtained in English-to-Japanese (Kanji) and Arabic-to-English (no merit this one, because the baseline was the only participant). Worst ranking results were for English–Thai, English-to-Tamil, English-to-Hebrew, English-to-Korean, English-to-Japanese (Katakana).

3 Conclusions

This phrase-based system based on standard Moses has been offered to the NEWS organizers to provide a reasonable baseline system for the competition. Also, it helps the participants to know the quality level of their systems compared to state-of-the-art transliteration when faced as a translation challenge.

In the next edition, we hope to provide an en-

Task	ACC	F-Score	MRR	MAP
ArEn	0.4809	0.9127	0.4809	0.1275
EnCh	0.1934	0.5850	0.1934	0.1830
ChEn	0.0098	0.6459	0.0981	0.0953
EnTh	0.0679	0.7069	0.0679	0.0679
ThEn	0.0914	0.7396	0.0914	0,0914
EnPe	0.4817	0.9060	0.4817	0.4482
EnHi	0.2700	0.7992	0.2700	0.2624
EnTa	0.2580	0.8116	0.2580	0.2572
EnKa	0.1960	0.7832	0.1960	0.1955
EnBa	0.2870	0,8359	0.2870	0.2837
EnHe	0.1090	0.7714	0.1090	0.1077
EnKo	0.2130	0.6177	0.2180	0.2176
EnJa	0.2091	0.7047	0.2091	0.2059
EnJk	0.461	0.6517	0.4611	0.2967

Table 3: Official NEWS 2016 Results.

hanced baseline system by tuning some parameters from the Moses system, and possibly competing in the shared task with some related approach to character-aware neural machine translation system (Costa-jussà and Fonollosa, 2016).

Acknowledgements

This work is supported by the 7th Framework Program of the European Commission through the International Outgoing Fellowship Marie Curie Action (IMTraP-2011-29951) and also by the Spanish Ministerio de Economía y Competitividad and European Regional Developmend Fund, contract TEC2015-69266-P (MINECO/FEDER, UE). Author also wants to specially thank Dr. Rafael E. Banchs for motivating these experiments.

References

Marta R. Costa-jussà and José A. R. Fonollosa. 2016. Character-based neural machine translation. In *Proceedings of the ACL*.

Chris Irwin David. 2012. Tajik-farsi persian transliteration using statistical machine translation. In *Proceedings of the LREC*.

Philipp Koehn, Franz Joseph Och, and Daniel Marcu. 2003. Statistical Phrase-Based Translation. In *Proceedings of the ACL*.

Philipp Koehn, Hieu Hoang, Alexandra Birch, Chris Callison-Burch, Marcello Federico, Nicolas Bertoldi, Brooke Cowan, Wade Shen, Christine Moran, Richard Zens, Chris Dyer, Ondrej Bojar, Alexandra Constantin, and Evan Herbst. 2007. Moses: Open Source Toolkit for Statistical Machine Translation. In *Proc. of the ACL*, pages 177–180.

Taraka Rama and Karthik Gali. 2009. Modeling machine transliteration as a phrase based statistical machine translation problem. In *Proceedings of the Named Entities Workshop: Shared Task on Transliteration*, pages 124–127.

Andreas Stolcke. 2002. Srilm-an extensible language modeling toolkit. In *Proceedings International Conference on Spoken Language Processing*, pages 257–286, November.

Author Index